# MISSING

## *The Search for My Son*

Vivian Churness

*- a true story*

Vivian

Churness

Missing
The Search for My Son


India Edition 2013
USA Edition 2014

ISBN: 978-0-578-14261-6

Portrait on back cover by Daniel Yu, Fotoby Studio, San Pedro, California



Indian edition published by: Ecumenical Book Services
152, Anna Salai, Chennai - 600 002, India.

E-mail ecubookservice@gmail.com

To Dave

and

In Memory of

Dr. and Mrs. Julius and Leela Savarirayan

Ranipet, South India

# Acknowledgments

My dear friend in India, Dr. Angeline Rajkumar, has encouraged me to tell my story so that others with similar experiences will know that they are not alone. Life has its ups and downs, and each of us has our own story to tell. I want to thank those who have helped me tell mine.

To those who read and discussed with me the first draft of this book four years ago—Derek Spring, Susan Saunders, Larry Christenson, Barbara Ponse, Carla O'Brien, Linda Howat, Angeline Rajkumar, Jenny Lowen, Joy Shepherd, and Micki, Barbara, and Adeline—thank you for your comments and suggestions. I want to thank Mr. K. V. Mathew of Ecumenical Book Services in Chennai, India who encouraged me and made this book possible. Mrs. June Hedlund, Mr. Isen Abraham, Mr. P. Raju, and Mr. Sathanam have all worked on this project. They are a good team with a passion for what they are doing.

A big thank you to Carrie Thompson, Dave Sheets, and others at Believers Press who helped in the creation of the American edition of this book.

My sisters Barbara Spring and Micki Miller, and friend Joy Shepherd have helped with the editing of the final version of this book. Colleen Ogden and Karen Grobien have assisted with proofreading, and my husband Dave has helped in every aspect of this project. Thank you.

I want to express my appreciation to Ann Zwemer, former missionary colleague with me in India in the sixties and still a dear friend. She not only helped me get started as an author, but also lived this story with me through the years. Her wisdom and advice has been invaluable.

And to all who read this book, I want you to know that God is with you. He will never forsake you.

Vivian Churness
March 2014

# Foreword

Vivian Churness writes a story that reads like a cross between a detective mystery and a testimony of personal spiritual formation. It is not an invented tale. It is the story of Vivian's search for her abducted son and the formation of her personal life during the years-long search. It is all true.

What does a young wife and mother do when her husband and three-year-old son suddenly disappear without a trace? Vivian and her husband have been separated for a year. The son was with his father when last seen. There have been no formal divorce proceedings and no question of child custody. The police say they cannot do anything; the boy is with his father. No friend or family member offers any hope or information. Private investigators can't turn up a clue.

Months and years go by. Every trail ends up a dead end. It would be easy for a mother to sink into a swamp of despair. Vivian went a different route: she pursued further education in her nursing profession and earned a PhD in Nursing Science. She found encouragement and support from spiritual comrades and in her church.

It was a privilege for me to serve as Vivian's pastor during much of this story. I won't ruin the suspense by telling you how it turns out. I encourage you to get into the book and start walking through the life and challenges of a remarkable woman — someone who said NO to despair, said YES to faith and hope, and said YES to forgiveness and love.

Larry Christenson

# Preface

This is a true story. I wish it were not.

Names of a few individuals have been changed to protect their privacy. For the most part, however, names, places, and dates are given as they occurred.

Vivian Anderson Hayes Churness

# Table of Contents

# 1
# A Day at the Zoo

We stopped the car on a quiet, shady, tree-lined street. No curbs or sidewalks. "This is the address," I said, looking around.

"Buz always liked living close to the beach," Greta added, and then shook her head in disbelief. "Why did he do this?"

We were just on the other side of Pacific Coast Highway in Laguna Beach, California. We looked at the house—an old, but well-kept, wooden structure in what was once a residential neighborhood with single-family dwellings. Now it looked like many of the homes on the street had been divided into smaller units to maximize rental income. Buz's street address was 370 ½; perhaps there was an apartment entrance in the back. My friend Greta and I were looking for my husband and son, or any clue to their whereabouts.

Buz and I had been separated for almost a year. Our three-year-old son, Philip, lived with me in San Pedro, and Buz lived fifty miles south of us. Today was a special day for Philip. He was going to spend the day with his father. Normally, I would have dropped Philip off at the babysitter on my way to work, but today I didn't have to do that.

It was early Thursday morning and Buz arrived at my apartment as planned.

"We're going to the Los Angeles Zoo. We'll be back in the afternoon," Buz informed me as I was getting ready to leave.

I kissed Philip good-bye and then smiled as I looked back and watched father and son sitting on the hardwood floor of my second-floor apartment playing with little matchbox cars. This is an image that would stay with me for years to come.

When I returned home from work at 5:30 p.m., they were not there as I had expected. I was worried, but there was not much I could do except wait. Buz had a habit of being late; nonetheless, I had a sick feeling in my stomach. I had been through this before.

After awhile, I picked up a book to read, hoping it would calm me while I waited. It was Kathryn Kuhlman's *I Believe in Miracles*, a book I had borrowed but never got around to reading. I sat near the telephone and read, getting up from time to time to look out the window to see if they were coming. It got dark outside—too late to be at the zoo; too late to be at a park.

As I neared the end of the book, I read the chapter about three little boys who had drowned in a lake. It was then I really became fearful that something may have happened to them, or more probably, Buz had intentionally taken Philip and didn't plan on returning. I called the police and told them what had happened. I told them my son was gone and my husband had taken him. They were not interested. "It's still early, ma'am. Your son is with his father. It's only 8 p.m. They'll be back in a few hours."

I sat down and finished the book. By now, I was sure they would not be coming home. In the past year, on several occasions, I had allowed Buz to take Philip to his home for an overnight or weekend visit. Each time Philip returned, he would be upset for a day or two. Because of this I stopped allowing Buz to take Philip for an overnight or weekend visit, but I encouraged and welcomed visits from him during the day. Recently Buz had asked if he could take Philip for an entire week—during his spring break from the elementary school where he was teaching. Because I said no, he might have just taken him—or they could have been in an accident.

I called the emergency rooms of several nearby hospitals and called the police again. There were no hospital admissions or police reports involving a man and a young boy—no one with the last name of Hayes. Furthermore, the police were not interested in filing a missing person's report, telling me, "The boy is with his father, they will be home by morning." I called Ruby and Norm McCauley, dear friends from church who knew us well. They knew how Buz had abruptly left me and were very concerned.

Ruby and Norm had been like surrogate parents to us from the time we were married five years ago. In fact, Buz called them Mom and Dad. But they had heard nothing from him for over a year now.

"Why don't you try calling the police again," they suggested, "and let us know what happens. We'll be praying for you."

I called the police several times, using different numbers listed in the telephone directory—the city police, the county police, the county jail, and every other number I could find listed. The result was the same each time: "There is nothing we can do to help you. He is with his father. Wait until morning."

I didn't sleep well. I was up very early in the morning and went to work an hour early, knowing someone would be there opening up the outpatient clinic. As I expected, Dr. Amil and Mary, his nurse, were there. Mary knew immediately that something was wrong. When I told her what had happened, she rushed me over to Dr. Amil, a tall, dark-haired man, standing at his office door, putting on a white lab coat and reviewing lab reports at the same time. He always reminded me of Desi Arnaz with his Latin accent and his love of playing jokes on people.

"Dr. Amil, Vivian's son is missing! Can you help her? Her husband took him yesterday and never returned."

At first he thought we were kidding him. Then, noticing the distressed look on my face, he could see it was not a joke.

Whenever I brought my son in for a doctor's appointment, we would stop in the internal medicine department and say hello to the doctors and nurses with whom I worked. They liked Philip. His big blue eyes, blonde hair, and ready smile never failed to charm them.

"Do you mean your husband took your child and didn't return?" He could see I was in a daze—not fully comprehending the situation. He looked straight at me and said slowly and deliberately, "Vivian, listen to me. Leave here and go to the police station! Right now!

Don't go alone," he added. "Do you have anyone to go with you?"

Within an hour, Ruby McCauley and I were at the Los Angeles Harbor police station in San Pedro. I told the police officer at the desk that my son was missing. As the waiting room was empty, several of the staff came over to listen as I told my story.

The officer at the desk wrote down some information, consulted with an officer standing behind him, and replied, "I'm sorry, there is nothing we can do to help you. The boy is with his father. This is Friday. They'll probably be back by Monday. No crime has been committed." The other officer nodded in agreement.

I knew in my heart that my husband and son were gone and not returning. But no one would believe me. The police explained that even if they did find them and took my son away from Buz, *they* would be the ones guilty of kidnapping.

They could do nothing.

We turned around and left, unsuccessful in convincing them to help.

Ruby stopped and looked at me. "Let's sit down and talk. You've got to go back and insist they do something. Vivian, you are too calm and rational and are protecting Buz. You're not telling them this is urgent. You're telling them his father loves him and would not harm him. Maybe some of that is true, but Buz is wrong because he didn't return Philip, and your son could be in danger."

Ruby knew me. I tend to be calm and quiet by nature. And, as a nurse, I have also been trained to remain outwardly calm and cool during emergencies. My training was not serving me well at this time. I was not outwardly emotional, but in this case I was worried sick and my stomach was like an empty pit. I was somewhat in a state of shock and not fully comprehending what had happened, but I realized I needed to speak up and fight for my child.

I went back to the police desk. I insisted and then begged them to do something.

This time they quickly escorted me into a room to speak with Janet, a detective in the children's division, who had been unobtrusively listening to the conversation at the desk. She looked like a social worker, a pleasant, mature woman dressed in street clothes. She questioned me further, and I again told what had happened. "Yes, we are married. We've been married for five years and living apart for almost a year. My husband filed for a divorce in December, and I requested counseling. He refused that and a hearing was set for June. No, there is no custody arrangement because we are still married.

"My husband had been agitated and disturbed in the past, and because his behavior was unpredictable, there were times when I would not allow him to take our son out of my sight. I believe he loves his son and would not intentionally harm him. I have no idea where he might have taken him, but I'm afraid my son is not safe."

She acted sympathetic but repeated the same words I had already heard, "There is nothing we can do. The boy is with his father. Come back Monday, if they're not home by then. In the meantime, I will send a report to the Police Department in Laguna Beach where your husband last lived."

It was Saturday and Greta and I were in Laguna Beach.

Greta knew Buz well and loved him. She and her husband, Bob Scott, were Philip's Godparents. Their teenage son had been in our church youth group when Buz and I were leaders a few years ago.

Greta and I walked to the back of the house where a tall wooden fence surrounded a patio area. The gate had been left open and we could see the glass patio doors, an entrance to the house. It looked like a small dog had been on the patio.

Yes, Buz could have lived here. He liked dogs. When we were together we had a Great Dane named Greta. I was dismayed when Buz named the dog after one of our best friends, but that's what he did. When we went our separate ways we gave the dog to a friend. Now it looked like he had another dog.

We tried the patio door and it opened. From the door we could look into the entire room. It was empty—completely empty except for some scattered bits of paper. A wall separated the room from the main house. We could see into a small bathroom. No one lived there. We stood there, but did not go in. Yes, Buz had lived here and had moved on.

All of a sudden, I was afraid! Something inside of me said, "Get out of here!"

I spoke up, "Let's leave!"

An empty feeling and a wave of grief replaced the fear. I sat in the car and said nothing.

After a few minutes of silence Greta asked, "What do you want to do next?" She was the driver and was willing to do whatever I asked.

We had been to the Laguna Beach Police Station earlier in the day. They were more willing to hear my story than were the police in San Pedro Harbor. They had not yet received a missing person's report but were willing to take a new one. An attractive young lady in her late twenties, dressed in street clothes, was standing at the side of the receiving desk listening to our conversation.

She introduced herself. "My name is Carlene. I'm a detective here with the children's division. I've been listening to your conversation and would like to help you. No crime has been committed, but something's not right here. You said the boy is with his father. Do you have legal custody of your son?"

"We're married. My husband filed for divorce several months ago, but there has been no legal separation, divorce, nor any custody arrangements."

She looked into my pleading eyes and said, "I am not authorized to take this case. But please come back on Tuesday and I will be here to help you. In the meantime, work with Harbor Detectives and have them send a report to us."

That was a few hours ago. Now we were sitting in the car wondering what to do next.

There was another lead to follow. I had the name and address of a babysitter, a woman who had taken care of Philip on a few occasions. It was on Pacific Coast Highway near La Strada Restaurant, where Buz worked as a waiter on weekends. We went to her address. After explaining who I was, she invited us in. Her own three-year-old son was playing in the living room.

"Yes, I took care of Philip a few times. I didn't know Buz well and don't know any of his friends. He dropped his son off here when he went to work and picked him up after work. I usually take care of several children in the evening. I'm sorry there is nothing more to tell."

Greta and I returned to San Pedro on the 405 freeway, exhausted and disappointed, but with a renewed sense of determination knowing that we were making progress. Back in San Pedro I made phone calls to people who knew Buz, hoping they could be of some help. Everyone I called seemed dismayed at what had happened and could or would not offer any helpful information.

Yesterday I had called the school where Buz was employed as a seventh grade teacher. The principal was shocked to hear what had happened and also angry.

"He called in sick yesterday and just didn't show up for work today. I'll ask the other teachers if they know anything."

I sat down to try to eat something when the phone rang. This was the call I was waiting for.

# 2
# Back to Laguna Beach

"Hello, this is Charles Jackson. I work with Buz at Franklin School. Is this Vivian Hayes?"

"Yes."

"I teach in another classroom, but I know Buz well. Our principal told me he has taken his son and hasn't returned. Is that right?"

I assured him that is what happened. He went on, "I have some information that may be of interest to you. Buz talked of taking his son and sailing to some island in the Pacific and getting lost forever. He said no one would ever be able to find them. He was studying navigation maps he had in his room. He's a good sailor and knows how to handle a boat. I thought he was just dreaming about this, but now I think that's what he might have done."

My heart sank. Yes, Buz was a good sailor. He had owned a Cal 20 sailboat before we were married, and after we were married he bought a Cal 25, a twenty-five-foot sloop. Just before Philip was born, we sold it, joking about trading the boat in for a baby. After that he hung out around marinas along the coast, getting to know boat owners.

When I had looked around Philip's room, only two things were missing: his teddy bear and his life jacket.

I called Douglas, my attorney who was already aware of the abduction, and updated him on all that had happened. He suggested I wait and see if they would return on their own. I wanted to do more than wait, but he said there was nothing he could do.

"As for 'sailing to an island in the Pacific and getting lost forever'—a lot of men fantasize about that, but never do it," he said.

I went to church Sunday morning with a heavy heart and somewhat in disbelief of my situation. My pastor, Larry Christenson, and others knew Philip was missing. A few mentioned they were praying for his safe return, but most said nothing. I went through the motions of the church service and spent the rest of the day with Greta and Bob.

I received a call from my attorney who was having second thoughts. "Yes, Buz may have taken your son with no plan of returning."

My parents, who lived in the Chicago area, were quite distressed. They wanted to come to California, but both my parents and I felt their presence might be a barrier to Buz coming home on his own. Also, they really did not have the money for the expensive airfare.

Monday morning Ruby and I returned to the Los Angeles Harbor Police Department and talked at length with the woman detective who had interviewed me on Friday. She had so many questions, and I answered the best I could. She suggested I talk with the Laguna Beach police again and let her know if anything further developed. She was very kind and thorough, but indicated to me again there was little they could do because the boy was with his father and there weren't any legal custody arrangements.

Now it looked like I was pretty much on my own in the search for my son.

I went to work for the rest of the day. The doctors and nurses in the outpatient clinic were very supportive and helped me to focus on my work. The hardest part was going home to an empty apartment. I felt hollow inside and many tears flowed. I tried to occupy myself by reading but couldn't concentrate on the words. I took a walk to visit a friend Anny, who lived around the corner. She was from Germany and had been through her own personal tragedies. She understood.

It was difficult to pray in any coherent fashion. My prayer was often just, "Help me! Jesus, help me!"

Tuesday morning I was back in Laguna Beach again with Greta. We stopped at the police station to see Carlene. She was waiting for us. She never did receive a report from the Los Angeles Harbor Detectives but, nevertheless, said she would go with us to Buz's apartment. She emphasized that she was not authorized to take the case, but would help me by providing backup as I searched. We met at the residence and I went in alone while Greta stayed in her car and Carlene circled the block. This time I went inside and was not afraid. The glass patio doors were still unlocked and everything was the same. I looked around—nothing in the closet. I picked up some pieces of paper with a few words in Buz's handwriting. Yes, he had lived here.

I went back to the car just as Carlene was driving by. I had another address I wanted to check out. When we moved from San Diego, Buz gave our piano to a friend of his who lived a few blocks from here. Carlene led the way to his house and we followed. I got out, again leaving Greta in the car while Carlene drove off remarking, "I'll meet you at the first address."

I could see the grand piano through the bay window. Yes, it was ours. We were still making payments, so it wasn't really ours, but there it was.

I knocked on the door. No answer. I went around the house and tried all the doors. They were all locked. No one was home and there was no way of getting in.

At this point, reality was so unthinkable that I let my mind put me in a different situation. Now I was beginning to feel like Nancy Drew! I was almost enjoying this. I loved to read Nancy Drew mysteries when I was younger. Now *I* was the girl sleuth.

We met Carlene back at Buz's apartment where she reported interviewing several of his neighbors. It was in an area where many gay men lived. They knew Buz and had talked with him, but he was not part of their community. She viewed that as something positive and said the neighbors had no information about him, nor had they ever seen a child with him.

One more place to go. Carlene departed and Greta and I went to La Strada Restaurant, where Buz worked part time.

"Yes, Buz Hayes worked here. If you like, you can come back at 4 p.m. and talk with one of the waiters who worked his shift."

We spent the next few hours at the beach, walking barefoot in the sand, sitting down from time to time to read, talk, and pray. It had been five days since my son had disappeared—a very difficult five days. Greta knew I needed a break so I could gain strength to keep on going. She was a beautiful woman, both inside and out, and always positive. Ten years older than I, she had been a mentor to me early in my married life. Buz often went surfing with her husband and son while we made dinner at her home. Now she was helping me keep my sanity in the midst of all of this.

At four o'clock we were back at La Strada, where we were escorted to a table and given a menu. After a few minutes a waiter came to our table.

"Are you Vivian, Buz's wife?"

"How did you know who I was?"

"You look just like your picture. Buz had a picture of you and Philip on his wall."

That struck both Greta and I as rather strange. When a man files for divorce, why would he want to keep a picture of his wife on the wall? I suppose it was because it was a picture of his son also. But then again, he could have found another picture of him.

After taking our order, the waiter came back to talk with us. He already knew why we were there and what had happened because Buz had discussed his plan with him. But Buz told him, "I'm not going to tell you where I'm going and when, because Vivian will get it out of you. She'll have a way of making you feel guilty so you will tell."

He said he had not been in touch with them since they left and he had no idea where they might have gone. We believed him.

In a couple hours we were back in San Pedro. As usual, on my way in, I opened my mailbox and retrieved my mail. There was a letter addressed to me in Buz's handwriting, postmarked, *Laguna Beach, CA*. The date was illegible.

# 3
# The Letter

I walked quickly up the stairs to my second floor apartment, and opened the envelope.

*Dear Viv,*

*Phil and I are taking a vacation. We shall be together. We both love you.*

*Love,*

*Buz and* [A scribble mark]

Today was April 7, 1970. I last saw them on April 2. The date on the postmark could not be deciphered, so I could only guess when it was mailed. Did Buz mail it himself or did he give it to a friend to mail?

I didn't know if the letter was good news or bad news. I got on the phone and called Ruby, then Greta. Then I cried.

How does one deal with not knowing? I still don't know the answer to this question. People have asked me how I coped with not knowing where they were, what was happening to my son, and if I would ever see him again. All I can say is that I just kept going. Others carried me through this. Friends, and even strangers, wanted to help. No one knew how to help, but they wanted to. That was enough. Somehow I got through each day.

Evenings after work were the hardest. There is a line in the Simon and Garfunkel song *Bridge over Troubled Water*[1] that talks about "when evening falls so hard." I knew exactly what that meant. Evenings were the hardest. I shed many tears when I walked into my empty apartment. I felt the emptiness more as it grew dark and I was alone.

My prayer over and over again was "Help me. Help me." And God did help me. He gave me peace, comfort, and yes, even joy, because I knew He was always with me. "I will never leave you nor forsake you"[2] was a Bible verse on the wall of my parents' bedroom. It is true.

One day, my pastor, Larry Christenson, suggested, "Now, Vivian, why don't you join us every morning for prayer. A few men and I meet in the prayer chapel at 6 a.m. daily. You can join us. It's just for half an hour. That way we will see you every morning, and you can tell us what you need and how we can help you. We can pray together and it will keep you from going around in circles."

From then on I met with the men each day before going to work. Every morning, except Wednesday, that is. On Wednesday the group was much larger. I didn't feel comfortable with that, so I skipped Wednesdays. About once a week, Bob Scott and one or two other men took me out for breakfast after our prayer session. I had to be a work at 8:30, so I was always the first to leave the restaurant.

I went to work every day and continued to make phone calls to anyone I thought might have any bit of information.

Nothing happened.

Harbor Detectives had no information for me. I considered having something put in local newspapers but decided against it. I did not want to do anything to make it more difficult for him to return on his own. I also considered the effect it would have on the children where he taught school. A newspaper article about a teacher abducting his son is not what I wanted at this time.

The next step was to see if he had obtained a passport for Philip. Norm McCauley drove me down to Los Angeles to the US government offices where I told the lady at the counter my story. Then I asked, "Has a passport been issued for Robert or Philip Hayes?"

She looked through a drawer, hesitated, looked up, and replied, "I'm not supposed to give you this information as it is confidential by law. I can't give you a copy but . . . I will tell you that a passport was issued to your son on March 20, 1970 and signed by his father."

"Did he say where they were going?" I asked.

"He put down something, but it wouldn't be of any use to you anyway. A person can put down anything he likes."

# 4
# Ports-O' Call

The passport was issued on March 20. That was three weeks before they disappeared. That was the day he came and took Philip for the day. "To a park," he said. They returned before I came home from work and were at the apartment waiting for me. Buz was often in a bad mood and abrupt with me when he came for Philip, but that day it was different.

Buz asked, "Would you like to go to Ports O' Call Village with us?" I still loved my husband and had hoped for a reconciliation, so I was happy to go with him.

Ports O' Call Village, a New England-style fishing village built to attract tourists, is about a mile from where I lived. We strolled along the oceanfront going in and out of the little shops. We bought ice cream cones. Then Buz bought a little bouquet of flowers and gave it to Philip to give to me. I began to have hope that we might get back together again. Little did I know this was part of the plan to gain my trust so I would allow him to take his son for another day.

In the past there were times when I did not allow Buz to take our son out of our house. These were the times when he seemed agitated and impulsive—not at all like the person I had married. However, because recently he was quite pleasant and seemed like his old self, I again allowed him to take his son out for the day. We enjoyed being together. I did not suspect that Buz was doing this for another reason.

I had been betrayed! This was not an impulsive act, but well planned. He knew right from wrong. How could he do this?

I called the office of my congressman and told a staff person my plight. Could he help me find my son? Surely he could be traced through his social security number, driver's license, or passport. Someone could find him. He said he would get back to me, but he never did.

I called several more times with the same response: they would get back to me. And they never did.

I tried to get information through the Internal Revenue Service. I learned that Buz did not pay taxes that year, which didn't surprise me. I could get no further information from them.

I thought of all the worst-case scenarios. Buz had been diagnosed with narcolepsy after sustaining a head injury in an auto accident. He seemed to be accident-prone and was frequently hitting his head on something. He was six feet three inches tall, so that was easy to understand.

The auto accident was seemingly a minor one in which he ran into the car in front of him. Buz was driving a borrowed convertible and carrying a surfboard in the back seat. The car in front of him stopped suddenly. Buz also stopped abruptly, sending the surfboard forward and hitting him in the head, which caused him to hit the car in front of him. There was only minor damage to both cars, but it left Buz in a daze. After that he had periods of confusion and frequent headaches. At times he fell asleep uncontrollably. It was impossible to awaken him when this happened. After sleeping a couple hours he was fine.

One day his supervisor at work called me and advised me to take him to a neurologist because he was not functioning well at work. He would need medical clearance before he would allow him to attend a workshop in another state.

The neurologist talked with us and explained that he had narcolepsy, a condition which causes a person to fall asleep uncontrollably. He probably had a brain contusion as a result of the accident, but seemed to have recovered from that. Buz was then given a prescription for a stimulant to keep him awake during the day.

When we were newlyweds, Buz was working as a chemist for a medical research lab, and then he got a job as sales representative with a pharmaceutical company. With both jobs he had access to medications—with or without a prescription. I was never sure what drugs he was taking. Once in a while he would confess to accidentally taking an overdose of something for a headache. His medical history was difficult to understand and somewhat bizarre. I talked with only one of his doctors—the neurologist.

Philip was about six months old when my husband switched jobs again, and we moved to San Diego. Some of the falling asleep and periods of depression continued.

After two years in San Diego we separated. It is hard to tell what led up to our separation. He announced one day that he would "crack up" if he stayed with me and outlined a plan for us to live separately in the San Diego area. Philip would live nearby with me. I suggested counseling, but Buz would not consider it. I talked with a mutual friend of ours who asked me the question, "Is he gay?" That had never entered my mind, but it gave me something to think about.

I consulted a lawyer, who suggested a medical evaluation for Buz. Within a month or two, we sold our three-unit building where we lived, paid off some debts and separated. I moved to San Pedro where we had both lived. And I could be back at the church where we were married. Buz went to Hawaii for a week or two. He said he had a job there modeling for a TV commercial. I'm not sure where he lived when he returned.

There was good reason for me to be concerned for Philip's safety. But I did know that his father loved him and was always good to him. When Buz was having difficulty at work and in life, he found great comfort in playing with his son.

I knew he would not intentionally harm him, but I was concerned that he would not be in a safe environment. And if Buz fell asleep uncontrollably, as he sometimes did, what would happen to Philip?

I often went to the verses of scripture in Matthew 18, "And whoever welcomes one such child in my name welcomes me."[3] Jesus also said children had special angels watching over them. I believed this and often thought of the verse, "Their angels in heaven always see the face of my Father in heaven." I truly believe Philip had special angels watching over him.

And I had my own angels watching over me. On more than one occasion, I saw a group of angels robed in white hovering over my head.

# 5
# The Do-Gooder

After my husband abducted our son, I was left with his debts. I was making payments on most of them until my attorney suggested, "Don't be too quick to pay off all of your debts. Most of them were incurred by your husband. Let the creditors try to find him. They have ways of finding people, and also, you may not be responsible for all of them."

I called every creditor and told them my story. One reduced my bill to almost nothing and told me he would help me search for my husband. The man later called back and told me his search was unsuccessful. At least he tried, and for that I was grateful and thanked him.

There was a downside to not paying Buz's bills. I received phone calls almost every evening asking for him. Some said they were bill collectors. Others, pretending to be friends, had all sorts of creative stories. I suspected some of them might have actually been from Buz or one of his friends. I had no way of knowing. Some would call and hang up. It got to be scary and unnerving. I considered changing my phone number, but I wanted to keep the same number in case I should ever receive a call with information about my son.

That fall, about six months after the abduction, I hired a private investigator from West Coast Detectives. My attorney had wanted me to do it earlier, but for various reasons I did not. One, of course, was the expense. I asked Ruby and Norm McCauley to be at my apartment when the detective came to interview me. Norm, an accountant who did taxes for a major aerospace company, was levelheaded. Ruby always had keen insight into behavior. Although she had gray hair and a wrinkled face, she was a person we often described as "ageless," because she was at ease with women of all ages, from young children, teenagers, and young mothers to middle-aged and older women.

Ruby and Norm were at my apartment when the detective came to interview me. I am glad they were there to keep me honest, as I tended to point out only Buz's good qualities. I wanted him to look good. Ruby and Norm reminded me that there was another side to him. He could be two different people. Overall, it was not a pleasant experience going through the interrogation.

At one point the detective told me, "You're a do-gooder and naïve."

He was right.

The detective pointed out that Buz had a key to my apartment. Why didn't I change the lock? I prayed that God would protect me. Now that I think back, I am sure the manager would have done so with minimal cost to me. Now I wonder whether I purposely did not change my lock, even though people felt I might not be safe from Buz. However, at the time, I was not concerned with my welfare, only of Philip's. In the back of my mind, I knew that if Buz used his key to get into my apartment, I would find out where Philip was.

Eventually I moved.

Christmas came and went. I thought they surely would come home for Christmas. When that did not happen, I realized that I might never see them again.

A sermon Pastor Christenson gave one Sunday morning stayed with me. It went something like this: "The worst thing in the world that could possibly happen has already happened. Jesus Christ, the Son of God was crucified. And he rose from the dead, victorious."

I had known and believed that since childhood. It is still true. I have nothing to fear. He is always with me and He has already won. I often thought of the verses in Romans 8 that I had memorized as a teenager.

> *For I am convinced that neither death nor life, neither angels nor demons, neither the present nor the future, nor any powers, neither height nor depth, nor anything else in all creation, will be able to separate us from the love of God that is in Christ Jesus our Lord.*[4]

# 6
# The Puppy

It was mid-January and already dark at 5:30 p.m. as I made my way home from work. I was driving my blue Plymouth around the bend on Western Avenue when a little dog appeared in front of me. Instinctively, I slammed on the brakes. At that moment I heard a loud *bang* at the rear of the car, as I was jolted back and forth. Then another jolt and another *bang*, not as loud as the first one. I sat there awhile, dazed, then opened the door and got out. A bystander came to help as the drivers of the other two cars were walking toward me. I was okay.

The driver of the third car remarked, "I was driving around the bend when I heard a bang. I looked around to see what had happened, and I hit the car in front of me."

No one was injured. My neck hurt, but I was able to move about and walk. I was guided to a gas station at the side of the road where I called the police. As no one was injured, the police did not come. I called a friend, Ella, who took me to Kaiser Hospital, where I worked.

After a visit to the emergency room, I returned home with a neck collar and some pain medication. I went to work the next day and the next. I am sure I was not much help in the clinic, but my coworkers covered for me.

One night the pain was severe enough to keep me awake all night. At 6:30 a.m. I finally went to the emergency room. I was back home before noon feeling great, thanks to the codeine I had been given. And a new, better-fitting cervical collar also helped.

When I arrived home, an insurance agent knocked on the door and asked if he could come in to settle the claim concerning the accident. Since he was from my own insurance company and I was expecting him, I invited him in. We discussed the accident and chatted for a while. It seems that we both grew up in suburban Chicago and our high school football teams had been rivals. Many good memories.

Then we discussed the insurance settlement. He noted that repair of the damage to my car was estimated at $350, the Blue Book price of the car. It was totaled. They would give me a check for $350, and I could have it repaired myself. That seemed fair. I signed something and he left. A few days later I received a check for $350 in the mail. I endorsed it under the words, "In full and final payment for accident occurring on January 20, 1971." I signed it and deposited it in the mail. The next day I called Douglas, my attorney, and told him what I had done.

"Go to the bank and get that check back! They may not have received it yet. Do what you can to get it back!"

I was now on sick leave from work, but I was able to drive to the bank that morning. I told the lady at the teller's window my story. Standing there with a cervical collar around my neck, I must have looked needy and a little forlorn because she immediately looked through a stack of envelopes on her desk and opened one.

"Yes, this is it. I have not yet deposited it. Here it is. You may have it. I know I'm not supposed to do this, but my brother is an attorney and he would have been furious had I signed and deposited a check like this. Good luck. Take care of yourself."

Almost a year later, I settled for a $10,000 payment from my insurance company plus the $350 for car repairs and all medical expenses paid.

I learned something from that experience: (1) Don't let a stranger into your home when you are alone, and (2) never sign anything important without having someone else look at it.

I think my guardian angels were working overtime.

The days went by with still no word about my son's whereabouts. Not one clue. Buz's mother and brother had no news. His mother had received a letter similar to mine at the time of their disappearance. The wording was the same, except it said, "We are going on a *long* vacation."

To say it was hard on her is an understatement. Her husband, Buz's father, had died two years prior to that. Buz went to Massachusetts for the funeral and was never the same after that. When he returned home he was depressed and had a few sessions with a psychiatrist, but he did not continue in therapy.

Buz's parents owned a hardware store, which his mother sold a year later. The loss of her husband, then the loss of her son and grandson, was extremely difficult for her. She wrote to me from time to time and we occasionally talked on the phone. The detective I had hired thought she might know something, but I didn't think she did—at least not at this point.

I enjoyed my job at Kaiser, and focusing on patients helped me as much as it did them. The doctors and staff I worked with were kind to me. They would ask a few questions to show their concern, and then say, "Now let's not talk about this anymore. It would be better to get your mind on something else."

# 7
# The Cloud

The months passed. They had been gone almost a year. I hoped for their return, but there had been no indication that they were even alive.

A turning point came for me one Sunday morning. Paul Anderson, our assistant pastor, at the close of the communion service remarked, "There are some here in our midst who are walking about in a cloud of grief. Let's pray for them."

Sitting in a pew, I broke down and sobbed. Many gathered around me and prayed; a few shed tears with me. It was an acknowledgment of my loss—like a funeral.

From that point on I was able to move ahead. I didn't know where *they* were. But I knew where *I* was. I thought, "If I ever do find my son, I don't want to be a basket case."

After that it was easier to make decisions. I wrote a letter to President Nixon:

*The President of the United States of America*
*The White House*
*Washington, DC 20012*
*Dear Mr. President,*

*I would like to appeal to you for assistance in locating my husband and son. On April 2, 1970, my husband* [Name and social security number here.] *took our three-year-old son Philip for a "day at the zoo." He is our only child. They never returned. In spite of my own efforts, efforts of the police and of detectives, of my attorney and of my husband's family, we have been unable to locate them.*

*My husband had left us the previous year because he felt he would "crack up" if he stayed with us. After this, he voluntarily saw several psychiatrists, but not on a regular basis. He told me he had been "close to suicide" on a number of occasions and he was very depressed. He had suffered a brain contusion and six brain concussions in various accidents since 1963. He seemed to be "accident-prone." In 1966 he was diagnosed as having narcolepsy and was told to take a stimulant drug to keep awake, especially when driving.*

*I am concerned about the safety of our son. … I later discovered that when they left he took with him Philip's teddy bear and his lifejacket. My husband loved to sail. He told a friend he wanted to sail to some island in the Pacific and get "lost forever." My husband was restless, however, and if he did do that, I feel he may be back in the United States or Mexico now.*

*At present, if something should happen to my husband, no one would know to whom the child belonged and he would be an orphan. At this point I do not know if my husband and son are even alive.*

*At the time of his disappearance last April my husband was teaching at. . . I was living with my son at my present address in San Pedro (Los Angeles Harbor). There were no custody arrangements, as I had hoped for reconciliation and that this would be only temporary. Whenever my husband saw a psychiatrist he would tell me about it and seemed to have some insight into his problems.*

*I have tried to locate him through Social Security Administration and through the Internal Revenue Service by myself and through my congressman. I have been told that any information of my husband's whereabouts is confidential by law and cannot be given to me. It can only be given out for humanitarian reasons. I appeal to you, Mr. President, that this be considered a humanitarian cause and that any information that would be helpful in locating them be made available to me.*

*Sincerely yours,*
*Vivian Hayes*

I decided to proceed with the divorce. Originally the court hearing had been set for last June, but after Philip was abducted I had it postponed. A new hearing date was set. My biggest fear was that I would not be granted custody of Philip, since, of course, I no longer had physical custody.

As my attorney and I entered the Santa Ana Courthouse, he assured me that I would not have to take the stand. He had spoken with my husband's attorney and briefed him on the circumstances. His attorney had not heard from Buz that past year, but would represent him anyway. He also had not been paid.

When the case was called the two attorneys met privately with the judge. But there was more. When they entered the courtroom I was told to take the stand. When they told me to take the stand, I was unprepared for what I might say. I didn't even know where to go or where to sit until someone got up and escorted me to a chair on a platform next to the judge.

The judge asked me, "When did you last see your son?"

I could barely get the words out of my mouth, "April 2, 1970."

He asked me a few more questions and then my attorney asked a few. I answered all of them, practically choking on the words.

Buz's attorney asked only one question, "Did your husband take good care of your son when he was with him?"

I answered a quiet, "Yes."

The judge wrote something down on paper while we all waited. "February 4, 1972. The dissolution of the marriage is granted. . . . Custody and control of the minor child Philip . . . (5 years old) is given to the Respondent (the mother). The matter of child support is reserved for adjudication at a later date."

I breathed a sigh of relief and joined my attorney at the back of the courtroom. On my way there, people in the courtroom waiting for another case got up and spoke to me. "We are so sorry. We hope you find your son."

I had dreaded this day. Now it was over. A victory, and yet an incalculable loss.

Now I could move on. I had to.

1967. Vivian, Buz and Philip
at age 5 1/2 weeks.

Philip at a birthday party at age 2 1/2.
The necklace is made of candy.
(Photo by Norma McCauley.)

1967. Vivian and Philip

1967. Buz sitting in a sailboat.

1967. Vivian and Philip with Dr. and Mrs. Julius and Leela Savarirayan on thier visit to San Diego, California. Dr. Savarirayan was Medical Superintendent of Scudder Memorial Hosptial, Ranipet, India when Vivian was there as a missionary 1960-1964. Buz took this photo.

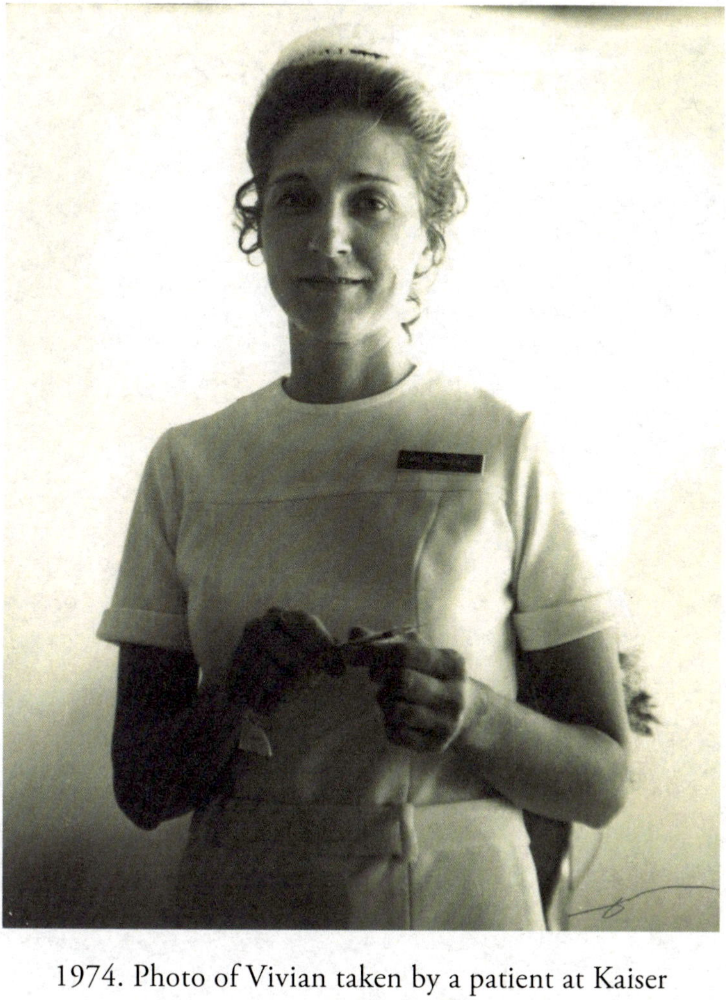

1974. Photo of Vivian taken by a patient at Kaiser Hospital, Harbor City, California.

# 8
# Choosing Life

Life went on. I decided to move from the outpatient clinic to the adjacent hospital where the work was more challenging. It was a good move and an easy one for me. I was assigned to a busy medical unit and interacted with the same group of physicians I had worked with in the clinic. Because I had worked in critical care in San Diego a few years prior to that, my skills were current. The nursing staff worked well together and we all looked forward to coming to work in the morning. The nursing care was excellent and there was a lot of laughter on the unit.

An added bonus was a more flexible schedule, which gave me time for ice-skating at the nearby Olympic Ice Arena, a few miles from the hospital. I started ice-skating by enrolling in group lessons. As a child I always wanted to learn to figure skate. When I was about twelve, my parents gave my sister, Adeline, and me a pair of figure skates for Christmas. Really nice ones! I say a "pair of skates" because we each received one skate—all my parents could afford at that time. We could never skate at the same time, but there were others to skate with. Every winter we would join the neighborhood kids, skating on flooded, frozen vacant lots. Now, as an adult, I could recapture those good times.

I had a routine of going to the rink at 5:30 a.m., skating for an hour, and changing into my uniform to report for work at 7:30 a.m. (This routine replaced the morning prayer meeting with the men.) After getting off work at 4:30, I went home, put a frozen dinner in the oven, set the alarm for forty-five minutes, took a nap, got up, ate, changed into my skating outfit, and headed for the rink for the evening. I took private lessons and got better. It was exhilarating.

I joined the college and career group at church. I was much too old for the group—over thirty-five, but they didn't seem to mind. I dated occasionally, but it really didn't interest me. It was too soon.

This was an exciting time at Trinity Lutheran Church, the beginning of the Jesus Movement with a youth group of about 350 on Wednesday evenings. There were children, teenagers, and young adults in every room, overflowing onto the patio. We had a dinner and confirmation classes for the children, and Bible study, singing, and prayer for the older group. Many of the guys in the older group had long hair and beards; the girls, too, had long hair and wore long cotton skirts. This, after all, was California. The counterculture hippie movement began slowly in different parts of the country and gained momentum in 1967 after young people from all over the country surged into the parks of San Francisco. Some who came to Southern California became believers in Jesus Christ and were baptized in the ocean. Many of these "Jesus people" were part of Calvary

Chapel in Costa Mesa, and some of them joined our group on Wednesday evenings.

Buz and I always lived near the ocean, partly because he liked to surf, but also because there was something about the counterculture lifestyle in the beach areas he liked. He was attracted to the hippie lifestyle, but never really became part of the group because he was too old, and of course, married. The hippies were mainly single people age twenty-five and under.

He seemed to have his affections in two camps. He was active in church but also wanted to be part of another lifestyle. He had been part of the early charismatic movement in Monterey Park and Monrovia in the early sixties and had experienced the gifts of the Holy Spirit. That is what brought him to the church in San Pedro where we were later married. There we were both active in prayer groups, Bible studies, and youth ministry.

But he also had another side. He spent a lot of time with friends in Hermosa Beach. Several times when we were invited to a dinner or party at the home of one of his friends, he cautioned me, "Don't drink the punch! There's cough medicine with codeine in it. And I'm not sure what else."

Or when cookies were passed, he'd look at me and quietly say, "Don't take any." Later he explained that they contained marijuana—all new to me.

Buz had one foot in each culture. By God's grace I was protected.

Now, here I was at age thirty-six, part of the Jesus movement, learning to play folk guitar, listening to Judy Collins's rendition of *Amazing Grace,* wearing a long dress, and, yes, a hairpiece to make my hair look longer than it really was. A favorite song of mine was:

God is so good.
God is so good,
God is so good,
He's so good to me.

In spite of all that had happened, I could say that God was good to me.

I visited my sister Micki in Connecticut and also stopped to see Buz's mother and brother who lived nearby. They had no news for me. His mother and I talked about how Philip would now be seven years old and about to finish the first grade. We were missing those years. The good news is that Buz's mother now had a boyfriend and was doing well.

I visited my parents and my other two sisters in my hometown of Harvey, Illinois. The people in the neighborhood literally received me with open arms.

The church at the end of the block, Bethel Reformed Church, was one I had attended as a child and teenager. It was still there and so were many of the people who had known me as a child, teenager, college student, and later as a missionary sent out by the Reformed Church in America to South India. It was good to be back in familiar territory. I kept thinking of the Bing Crosby song from the late forties, "I love those dear hearts and gentle people from my hometown."[5]

The bad news was that my father was diagnosed with lung cancer. After surgery and radiation therapy, he did quite well and was able to take some short trips with my mother. But it made me realize that, perhaps, now was the time for me to move back to the Midwest.

# 9
# Notre Dame

I was at home one evening reading *Escape from Loneliness* by Paul Tournier.[6] He told the story of a woman, living alone, who turned on the radio every evening just to hear a human voice say, "Good night."

I thought, "That's me! Here I am, sitting alone in my apartment talking to the TV!"

I longed for the days when I came home to a person. When I was growing up there was always someone at home. In college and nurses training, I lived in dormitories with plenty of activity. Later, as a missionary in India, I was rarely alone. Now I was living by myself. Living in a college dormitory was a memory of the past. Or was it?

I would have been content to be a wife and mother and never return to school. But that is not the way it happened. And not the way either of us had planned it. Buz and I were happy our first year of marriage. We both worked and did a lot of fun things together when we were not working. Problems didn't surface until I became pregnant and had a child. The new responsibilities, reduced income, and other factors were too much for our marriage to survive intact.

Now I was single again with no one to care for except myself. It was an opportunity to go back to school. Even before the divorce was final, Douglas, my attorney, had encouraged me to explore the possibility of getting an advanced degree.

I applied to the master's program in nursing at the University of Michigan and requested a Federal Nurse Traineeship grant. These grants paid tuition and fees plus a monthly stipend. I received a quick response.

> *We regret that the US Congress and the present administration has rescinded funding for Nurse Traineeships at this time. We ask that you write to your State Representative in Washington and to President Richard M. Nixon and request that they be restored.*

"That's not going to help *me*," I thought.

I considered a different approach. Perhaps I could do graduate work in psychology. My BA at Hope College was in psychology. I could do that, and somehow apply it to nursing. I thought of the University of Notre Dame in South Bend, Indiana.

The university is an easy two and a half-hour drive from my parents' home in Illinois. It was a Catholic university, but I was comfortable with that, as I had many close relatives who were Catholic. Attending mass with them on various occasions was always a positive experience. I had also read a book by Father Edward D. O'Connor telling of a spiritual renewal at Notre Dame. It was a prestigious university with high academic standards. It was worth a try.

I applied to the doctoral program at Notre Dame and designated psychology as my major. Within that field I chose gerontology, as it seemed to best match my prior experience in nursing. I had to take the Graduate Record Exam (GRE) to complete the application. Before I took the exam I arranged for special tutoring in math. My sister Barbara, a seventh grade math teacher, also helped me with what was then called the "new math."

I remember her comment, "Vivian, you don't even know the *old* math!" Nevertheless, I was highly motivated and continued.

I read through an introductory psychology textbook. I enjoyed studying again and was excited to be able to take the test at a nearby university. Even if I was not accepted, it had been fun preparing for the GRE.

I was accepted in the PhD program in psychology and was granted an assistantship. That meant full tuition, plus a stipend for room and board. In exchange I would be working with Professor John F. Santos.

In August of 1974, four years after the abduction, I bade farewell to my friends in California and boarded a plane for Indiana. It was a strange feeling. I had no keys! No car key, no house key, nor keys to anything else—just a suitcase. My furniture would come later and be stored at my sister's home.

I stayed the first night in a hotel in South Bend. The next morning I took a taxi to Lewis Hall on the campus of Notre Dame. The taxi driver, a football player who arrived on campus early for football practice, took me on a guided tour of the campus before dropping me off at my destination. Wanting to know more about me, he asked, "Are you a nun, or are you divorced?"

I thought that was a rather strange question. Obviously, I was not right out of high school.

Lewis Hall was formerly a dormitory for nuns attending graduate school. When it was built, the "religious" were the only women in an all-male school. More recently the university had become coeducational. But, even now, the majority of students were men. Women traditionally went to Saint Mary's College across the highway.

College life was a huge culture shock for me. It had been fifteen years since I was in school. I was also used to life-and-death matters in a hospital. On campus a major crisis was when the marching band showed up at the wrong place. To them it was like a Code Blue and was reported in the college newspaper as if it were a major disaster.

In the hospital I prayed for people who were sick. Here I prayed that I would pass my exams. I was used to dressing neatly in the latest fashions. Graduate students did not have time for that. The look could best be described as, "I don't care what I look like as long as I get this paper in on time." I soon fit in with the rest.

A big thrill for me was hearing the marching band practice. The strains of "Cheer! Cheer for old Notre Dame"[7] would excite all of us as the band marched past the psych building on the way to the stadium. A quick survey of the students in the classroom revealed that all of us had played in high school bands.

My classmates were mostly young men. We sometimes studied together in the library of Haggar Hall, the psych building. I was raised in a family of four girls, and being in a department with mostly guys was a new experience. I was usually the only woman in the group. We chatted as we studied, the conversation revolving around three topics—sports, women, and psychology, in that order. I mostly listened. The guys were smart and helped each other rather than compete. I didn't think I would survive, but I did, just barely.

Almost all undergraduate students lived in residence halls on campus: two for women and the rest for men. A priest or nun, serving as rector, resided in each hall. Living in the same residence hall all four years contributed toward a sense of community and belonging. There were no fraternities or sororities.

Residence halls competed with each other in athletic events. Open spaces on campus quadrangles were often filled with men and women practicing some sport. Mostly it was Frisbee throwing between classes. On my way to Haggar Hall or the dining hall, I often dodged Frisbees, lest I get hit.

The undergraduate students ate in dining halls while graduate students were on their own for food. Many of us ate in the "pay caf" (the pay cafeteria) in the center of the campus. I often sat at the table of Dr. Anton-Hermann Chroust, a retired professor of law who had written books on Aristotle, Socrates, and other philosophers.

Professor Chroust, a distinguished looking, white-haired man with a German accent, arrived at the pay-caf about 5 p.m. and usually stayed for a couple of hours. Graduate students, priest, nuns, and people like myself would join him for lively conversation about philosophy, law, religion, and topics like sports cars and driving 100 miles an hour on the German Autobahn.

He introduced students to each other as they came and went. He became my confidante on legal matters concerning my missing son.

Notre Dame was a good place for me to be at that time. My work with Professor John Santos consisted of helping with a Mental Health Outreach Program for the Elderly. The program consisted of training "younger" older people to work with the frail elderly. It was a good fit for me and got me into the community of South Bend. I also assisted with his undergraduate psychology classes by arranging for students to do volunteer work in nursing homes. I was in my comfort zone in that area.

The best part of my two years at Notre Dame was the people I met. As a grad student in gerontology, I often gathered with others at the home of Dr. Santos. We called him "Papa John"—but not to his face. It was at his home that I met Father Henri Nouwen. He and Dr. Santos had both worked at the Menninger Clinic in Topeka, Kansas. When Dr. Santos started the Psychology Department at Notre Dame, he brought Father Nouwen with him to start the Department of Pastoral Theology.

I recall the afternoon Father Nouwen spent with our mental health outreach trainees. He "accidentally" left his briefcase with his lecture notes back on campus. So he just talked from his heart on Curing vs. Caring.

"We Americans want all illness to be cured," he said. "We want perfection. We must accept the fact that we can't always cure. But we can always care."

Later, Dr. Santos explained it like this: In America we like to set goals. Then we either reach them or fail to reach them. Instead, we need to think of a target and try to get as close to it as we can. He told me of a graduate student who got the highest grade on a test in his class, yet was crying when she learned of her score.

"Why are you crying?" he asked.

"Because it wasn't a perfect score."

He explained that we sometimes overbuild our expectations and commit to perfection. We need to set a target and get as close to it as we can. "I will do my best" is enough.

A favorite Henri Nouwen story told by John Santos is when Henri arrived to stay at his home with nothing except the clothes on his back. He had given his money and clothing to some needy person along the way. Mary Alice

(John's wife) had to go out and buy him something to wear during his stay with them. Henri was known to be a person whose priorities were different than most of us.

I corresponded with Dr. Elisabeth Kübler-Ross while I was at Notre Dame. She lived near my hometown in Illinois and was kind enough to encourage me in my studies. I had written to her when I was in California, telling her I had read her book *On Death and Dying* and that my own experiences as a nurse validated her observations. I told her I would be attending Notre Dame soon. She responded immediately and introduced me to a professor on campus. We corresponded again after that, but I was never privileged to meet her in person.

Toward spring we had an influx of strangers on campus. Students talked of men wearing new "Farmer John" overalls checking on maintenance in the dorms. New faces appeared in the library on campus. Men punched the button for the fourteenth floor when they entered the elevator. (No one ever went to the top floor, as that was Father Hesburgh's penthouse.) It didn't take long to figure out they were Secret Service Agents preparing for an upcoming visit by President Jerry Ford.

The Vietnam War had ended and Nixon had resigned amidst the Watergate scandal. This was a new chapter in American history.

I was seated in the front section of the Athletic and Convocation Center when President Ford spoke to the student body. I don't remember what he said, but I do remember secret service men standing in front facing the president and another group facing away from him. They were everywhere, constantly scanning the audience and looking like they were ready to jump into action at any second.

Ford was not president for long. The following year, President Jimmy Carter was the guest speaker at graduation. This time I opted to participate in the event from outside the building.

My father was very ill with lung cancer when I arrived at Notre Dame. I was glad I had made the move, as it enabled me to go home from time to time. His condition gradually declined until he died in April before the end of the academic year.

The loss of my father, in addition to the loss of my son and husband, was almost too much for me to bear. God knew that and comforted me. He was with me.

# 10
# Circling the Globe

I commented to a friend at Lewis Hall, where I lived, that "Life is hard!" She encouraged me to see a counselor and recommended Dr. Morton Kelsey, an Episcopal priest and professor in the Department of Education. I already knew him, so I didn't hesitate to make an appointment. After listening to me, he suggested I have regular sessions with a counselor at the Family and Children's Counseling Center in Mishawaka, a neighboring town. I did and I benefited more than I believed possible.

In the following weeks I sometimes had lunch with Morton Kelsey and his wife in the pay cafeteria. Dr. Kelsey was very much into the psychology of Carl Jung. Jung identified universal symbols and recurrent themes or archetypes occurring in different cultures throughout time. He remarked that the image of a mother and a lost child was one of these. Somehow, it was comforting to me knowing that I was not the only one who has ever searched for a missing child. I have since learned that just knowing you are not alone in an adverse or trying experience makes one feel a part of a community rather than feeling so alone. I was one of many throughout the ages. Perhaps I was atypical, but certainly not the only one who had gone through the unthinkable for any parent.

Also a comfort to me was knowing that every mother eventually loses her child. The time comes when every mother has to release her child and let him go; mine just came sooner than most.

I continued to do what I could to find my son. I sent a letter to Betty Ford similar to the one I had sent to President Nixon. I guess I thought I would get a better response appealing to the president's wife. This time I got a little further with it. A new law, The Privacy Act of 1974, now allowed me to have information pertaining to my minor son. I received a letter from the Commissioner of Social Security stating a search of my ex-husband's social security file revealed that no survivor's claim had been made. In other words, his social security account was inactive, but there was no indication that he had died. This gave me a valid reason to continue my search, even though some of my well-meaning friends had told me to assume Philip was dead and go on with my life.

I wrote a letter to Father Hesburgh, the president of the University of Notre Dame, and tried to make an appointment to see him, but I never got past his secretary. However, I did receive a response from the General Counsel of the University who put me in touch with the County Prosecuting Attorney. Also, in response to his request, I received a letter from the FBI reporting that they had no file on my ex-husband. They explained this simply meant he was not being investigated for any federal offense. Not much came of it, but it was a step in the right direction.

When Jimmy Carter became President of the United States in 1977, I wrote to him. Also, I sent a letter to Senator Edward Kennedy, a friend of Father Hesburgh. I received a personal letter from Senator Kennedy telling me he had referred the matter to Senator Birch Bayh of Indiana. This was soon followed by a letter from Senator Bayh, promising to do all he could to help me. Finally, prominent people were hearing my pleas and making an effort to help.

Eugene, my therapist at the Family Counseling Center, not only counseled me but also helped me to contact the Department of Welfare to ask for help in locating my ex-husband for nonpayment of child support. The Federal Parent Locator Service Laws had recently been passed, allowing social security numbers to be used to locate absent parents. Even though the matter did not involve child support payments, with Eugene advocating for me, they accepted my application.

"What about the Salvation Army?" someone suggested. "Don't they have a missing persons service?"

Yes, they did. I talked with a Salvation Army worker on the phone. Even though willing to help, they were not optimistic about finding them. So much time has gone by, and children change so much. (Philip would now be nine years old.) Nevertheless, they put a missing person's ad in their magazine *The War Cry*. The ad read, "Missing, Nine-year-old boy, blonde hair, blue eyes traveling with his father. Call 1-800 . . ."

The real breakthrough came when a staff person at Notre Dame referred me to the local Women's Advocacy Center. There I talked with Sharon, an attorney who was willing to take my case.

Within a few months she called me into her office with good news.

"I have a copy of your son's passport here. I was able to secure it with the help of Congressman John Brademas from Indiana. The Privacy Act of 1974 now gives you access to information concerning your minor child."

She handed me a copy of Philip's passport. It had a picture of him with Buz's signature dated March 20, 1970, the same date given to me by the clerk in Los Angeles. The destination listed was "Germany and Spain."

Follow-up inquiries by my attorney, working through Congressman Brademas, revealed that it was not likely that Buz was in Germany since he had not applied for a visa, nor had he renewed his passport with the American Consulate in Germany.

The Ambassador of Spain wrote that it was quite possible he could be in Spain, as a visa was not needed for American tourists to travel within the country. He could have entered and stayed without further registration.

Sharon also contacted the US Passport office on my behalf and learned that their passports had not been renewed. I then requested they mark my son's passport with a note that I was the custodial parent and I was to be notified if anyone attempted to renew it.

I seemed to be getting help from many sources now, for which I was grateful. It gave me the most hope I had since Buz disappeared with Philip.

Sharon, my attorney, had been a good advocate for me. As I left her office for the last time, she said to me, "and one more thing, if you should get married again—be careful!"

That advice stuck with me.

I graduated from Notre Dame in 1976 with a Master of Arts in Psychology and decided not to pursue a doctorate in that field. A doctoral degree in nursing is what I really wanted. I loved being a nurse, and it didn't seem prudent to change professions.

In the fall I was offered a full-time faculty position in the Department of Nursing at Saint Mary's College, a college of the Sisters of Holy Cross, which I accepted. Although it was my first experience teaching in a Bachelor of Nursing Science program, I knew immediately that it was what I wanted to continue doing. Students took courses at both Saint Mary's and Notre Dame and had the benefit of being part of both communities. I, too, participated in activities on both campuses.

With the new position came an opportunity to represent the college at a conference of the International Congress of

Nurses in Tokyo. In the summer of 1977, I flew to Tokyo, then to Bangkok for a week's stay with a former Hope College roommate, then on to Dhaka, Bangladesh, where I visited the Sisters of Holy Cross. From there I flew to South India for a month long visit at the hospital where I had formerly served as a missionary.

On my way to Madras, I stopped in Calcutta to see friends I had known years ago in South India. They took me to see an orphanage where Mother Teresa was caring for young children.

Unfortunately, Mother Teresa was in New York City, so I didn't get to meet her. But we did meet some of the nuns who were caring for about thirty children. It was in a small dormitory-type building with cribs, beds, and open spaces. Outside the gated compound was a smelly trash heap with people digging for food or items to sell. Flies were inside and outside of the building. In spite of the environment, the children were being cared for lovingly. Yes, Mother Teresa chose one of the worst places to locate an orphanage—where it was needed most.

I flew to Madras (now Chennai) where I was met by friends I had known in the sixties. Soon I was back home at Scudder Memorial Hospital in Ranipet, where I had served as a missionary-nurse for a little over four years.

It was now 1977, thirteen years since I had left India to marry Buz. Much had happened since then. But now I was thinking about a more pleasant time.

# Missing

I met Buz in 1958, the beginning of my senior year at Hope College. We dated and were quite serious about each other, but I felt called to be a missionary in India, and he had more years before he would complete his education. Because he was pre-med, hoping to go to medical school, we went our separate ways. After graduating and teaching at my alma mater, Presbyterian St. Luke's Hospital School of Nursing in Chicago, I was sent out as a missionary to India by the Reformed Church in America.

They were happy years and fulfilling both personally and professionally. So much so that I have, to this day, not severed my ties with India's nurses.

After I had been in India for three years, I started corresponding with Buz. He was now in California, had completed his Bachelor of Science degree, and had a good job. Eventually he proposed by mail and we were engaged the same way, by intercontinental letters. I left India in December 1964, knowing I would never see most of my friends again until we all met in heaven.

Buz and I were married four months later. I wish I could say "and we lived happily ever after," but you know that is not what happened. Now it was thirteen years after I thought I would never return to India, and I was sharing my sad story with my dear friends, who grieved with me. Most were already aware of what had happened through correspondence.

It was good to renew friendships. I was pleased when Dr. Beulah Baskar, a staff obstetrician and gynecologist said, "Vivian hasn't changed one bit. Same personality—and she still has the same walk."

In the sixties there had been six to eight American missionaries at the hospital and mission schools in Ranipet. Now Miss Dora Boomstra, a teacher and school administrator, was the only Reformed Church in America (RCA) missionary in the Vellore-Ranipet area. Indira Gandhi was now the Prime Minister and things had changed. (When I arrived in India in 1960 Nehru was Prime Minister followed by Shastri at the death of Nehru in 1964. )

I loved India. I loved the rural Ranipet area where we could take evening walks and look at a million stars in the sky, amazed that the Big Dipper was upside down in India. At night, as we slept on the screened-in verandas, we could hear the wheels of bullock carts slowly turning. Mostly, I loved the people, always warm and welcoming.

Before I left Ranipet, Dr. Baskar gave me the names and addresses of nurses I had formerly taught who were now in the Persian Gulf. I would soon be visiting missionaries in those countries; seeing my former students was an unexpected bonus.

From Ranipet I went to New Delhi to visit a dear friend, then on to Muscat, Oman, and Kuwait. From there I flew to Italy, where I visited the Saint Mary's College campus in Rome, then to Geneva to visit the offices of the

International Council of Nurses and the International Red Cross Headquarters. This was my last stop before returning to the USA via New York. I had circled the globe in two months.

Everywhere I went I looked for an eleven-year-old, blonde-haired, blue-eyed boy. I knew it did not make sense, but I looked for him everywhere I went. Of course, I didn't find him, but I satisfied myself that I was not ready to return to India or any other country as a missionary. I had considered the possibility of going out again as a missionary, but now I knew I could not do it until I found my son.

# 11
# Indiana University

When I heard a doctoral program in nursing had been started at Indiana University in Indianapolis, I applied for a faculty position there and was accepted. It was expected that traineeships for the doctoral program would soon be available, and I wanted to be the first to hear of them.

Another move. This time to a newly built apartment complex just west of the interstate highway circling Indianapolis. The main campus of Indiana University (IU) was in Bloomington. The School of Nursing, part of the Medical Center campus in central Indianapolis, was fifty miles north of Bloomington. Outside of the interstate circle were new housing developments and a few large shopping centers, but mostly fertile farmland. This was Central Indiana and a very different culture from South Bend in the northern industrialized part of the state.

The commercials on TV were mostly for farm equipment and fertilizers. A typical date for me was to a tractor pull and State Fair (fun) or watching the trial runs of the Indianapolis Speedway races (exciting). The Speedway races brought lots of party people into town. Enterprising locals living around the Speedway rented out their front lawns as parking lots. Nurses could always work extra hours through registries to bring in extra money.

I attended a local church and got to know a few people, but mostly I spent time with my coworkers.

Faculty meetings at the IU School of Nursing were different from any I had ever experienced. I had taught at Presbyterian-St. Luke's in Chicago, Scudder Memorial Hospital in India, St. Joseph-Benton Harbor Community College in Michigan, and Saint Mary's. We never had more than ten or twelve attend a faculty meeting at any of these schools. At IU there were 120 nursing faculty members present at the first meeting I attended. This included all nursing programs in the Indiana University system throughout the state. They were all under one dean, Betty Grossman. She was a tough lady, yet very gentle. Sort of reminded me of an old-fashioned head nurse who loved what she was doing—a good administrator as evidenced by the success of the school.

Before the academic year was over, I had applied to the doctoral program at IU, and like other students in the new program, received full funding. In exchange, I worked for Carol Deets, my major professor. My job was to help other students analyze data for their research projects using a statistical software package I had learned to use at Notre Dame.

Carol was a gifted teacher and a role model for me. I have a picture of Jesus sitting on a rock, teaching a crowd of people of all ages. "And He taught them" was the caption. Whenever I see that picture, I always think of Carol Deets.

On November 22, 1978, the news on TV was all about Jim Jones and the suicide of nine hundred Americans in Guyana, South America. Their leader, Jim Jones, had brainwashed his followers into drinking a sweet liquid laced with poison. Pictures of bodies were all over the TV screen. Entire families with children were dead. As the story unfolded, we learned that some of the people tried to get away. But most willingly followed their leader to their deaths.

When the bodies were shipped to Dover Air Force Base in Delaware, my first thought was that my ex-husband and son could be among them. Buz was overly religious at times. I saw him being excited about faith in God and Jesus, and then faith in food supplements, bodybuilding, anabolic steroids, and then other drugs. He started out seeking to better himself and was led in different directions at different times. He often followed a strong leader, got excited with his teachings, only to later find fault with him and turn away. Then he would become excited about something else. Buz easily could have been one who followed Jim Jones. I hoped not, but I had to consider the possibility that he might have gone to Guyana with him.

I sent a letter to the address flashed on the TV screen and gave details of my son and ex-husband. I asked that I be notified if they were among those who were in Guyana at the time. I was relieved when I did not hear from them.

Jim Jones was from a small town near Indianapolis. People knew him and wondered, "How could this have happened?" It was a sad Thanksgiving weekend. On TV, Tom Brokaw quietly commented, "How frail is the human existence."

Yes, we are all frail and broken.

I remember the sermon that Sunday morning. The pastor spoke about what had happened and addressed the unspoken concern of many.

"Could that happen to me? Would I follow someone like Jim Jones?"

He assured us that we would not. Not if we follow the Good Shepherd and listen to His voice. "His sheep follow him because they know his voice. But they will never follow a stranger."[8]

I moved into the dormitory with a roommate, Alice, a student in the undergrad program. Recently divorced, she was starting all over again training as a registered nurse in the two-year Associate Degree program. I knew she would be a good nurse. She was bright, emotionally mature, and had the speed and agility of a dancer. (She had been a ballet dancer until she injured her knee.) Her husband had worked in the auto industry and lost his job in the recent recession. His unemployment and subsequent depression led to the divorce.

Alice was much younger than I, but we were good roommates. She deferred to my age and took the top bunk, allowing me to sleep on the bottom. Our diet was typical of most students— peanut butter and crackers, apples, popcorn, water, and an occasional meal in the cafeteria. Sally, a classmate in the doctoral program, invited Alice and me to a Sunday morning brunch at a home where Lillian Carter, the mother of the president of the United States, was to be the guest of honor. Sally, who was active in national politics, was unable to attend and had asked us to represent her.

When we arrived, the host, who graciously invited us into his beautiful, spacious home greeted us. We told him we were especially happy to meet Mrs. Carter, knowing she was a nurse who had served in the Peace Corps in India. I too, had served in India as a nurse-missionary.

I am sorry to say, what impressed Alice and me most was the food. Beautiful food was set out on the buffet table: egg dishes, sausages, rolls, pastries, fresh strawberries, pineapple—you name it. We had not seen that much food in a long time. We looked at each other with a smile as we determined not to pig out. We later had many laughs about that. Such is the life of a student.

During the brunch I went over to Mrs. Carter, a vibrant, peppy, white-haired woman in a lavender polyester pantsuit, sitting in a chair waiting to greet visitors. I waited my turn and then talked with her for a while about India. I did not ask for an autograph, as others did, as it would have spoiled our conversation.

That year I worked on the campaign to reelect Senator Birch Bayh. He had been responsive to my request for help and I wanted to show my appreciation. I helped by writing short notes, stuffing envelopes, and making phone calls. Senator Bayh came to thank us, and I shook his hand. His wife had recently died and he was wearing a wedding ring. Ronald Reagan won the presidential election that year (November 1980), and Bayh lost to Dan Quayle. Another chapter in history.

It was about that time that I received a letter from the deputy prosecuting attorney in Indianapolis directing me to make an appointment with the Parent Locator Service and renew my application to find my son's father. I am not sure if this came because of the efforts of those in South Bend or the efforts of Senator Bayh. When I talked with a social worker, she directed me to contact the police department in Indianapolis and request that they reactivate my missing person's case in the search for my son. I contacted them and was told that I must do this through the Harbor Detectives of the LA Police Department, where I had made the initial report.

I contacted Harbor Detectives and asked that they reopen the case. They later telephoned and explained that they had no record of the incident and no report could be found. They asked if I had a case number or report number. I did not. I had never thought of asking for one at the time. Now I am wondering if they ever filed a formal report.

Several months later I had good news. I received a letter from the prosecutor's office saying they had found a Robert Hayes at an address in Glendale, California. Since Glendale is about thirty miles from where we once lived, an area familiar to Buz, it sounded credible.

# 12
# California

I called Maureen, a friend in South Bend, to tell her the good news.

"Let me get you an airline ticket," she said. "You can fly out of South Bend. I'll put it on my credit card and you can pay me later."

Maureen was divorced with three children and could empathize with me. And she knew I didn't have a credit card.

A few hours later she called back. "We have a ticket for you to leave Wednesday from South Bend. If you can drive up tomorrow, you can stay overnight and we'll take you to the airport in the morning."

Soon I was on my way to Los Angeles. In the seat next to me was a middle-aged man who greeted me with a smile. He introduced himself as a pastor.

We chatted for a while. When he asked me where I was going, I told him a little of my story and informed him of my good news. My son would now be thirteen years old and I was on my way to California to check out the address.

We conversed a little longer and he said, "You know, it may not be your ex-husband and son. What will you do then?"

I hadn't considered that. I wanted to believe it would be them.

"I will be praying for you," he said.

Now that I look back, I wonder if he could have been an angel.

The McCauleys and their nineteen-year-old granddaughter, Belinda, drove me to Glendale. It was about a block from Forest Lawn Memorial Park in a well-kept neighborhood. Our plan was to have Belinda go to the door carrying a bag of cosmetics, ring the bell, and announce she was selling beauty products. She would ask for the lady of the house and engage the person in conversation while looking around to see who might be living there.

We parked across the street from the house while she boldly approached the front door. After a short conversation she returned to the car looking disappointed.

"No, Buz isn't there. The man looked like he was Mexican. He said he had lived there five years and no one by the name Hayes lived in the neighborhood."

I was disappointed, but prepared for it. Norm took us all out to lunch and we returned home. Actually, it had been a good day and I was happy to be back in California. At least there had been some action, and I had a chance to be with the McCauleys again.

Now what?

After returning to Indianapolis I hired another private investigator to check out the address in Glendale. I talked with the detective by phone and sent them the information I had, along with a check. A month later I received the final report. They had spent many hours sitting in a car near the address, watching people come and go at different hours. There was no evidence that Buz had ever lived at that address. They did find a man with the same name at a different address, but it was not Buz.

# 13
# Mississippi

With my Doctor of Nursing Science degree in hand, I graduated from Indiana University. Later the name of the degree was changed to Doctor of Philosophy, so I could use either designation. The important thing to me was that it was in nursing.

I went for job interviews at Georgetown University in Washington DC and at the University of Southern Mississippi in Hattiesburg near the Gulf Coast. The cost of living in Washington was quite high and the salary offered not as good as the University of Southern Mississippi (USM), so I took the position in Hattiesburg. At times I wondered if I had made a mistake in not accepting the offer to teach at Georgetown. But later events would show that it was not a mistake.

The first thing I noticed on the USM campus was that the students were very polite. It was "Yes, ma'am" or "No, ma'am" and "May I help you?" Walking about on campus, I rarely had to open a door for myself as there was always a young man moving quickly ahead of me to hold it open. This was the culture of the South.

People were good to me. Yet, in spite of having friends at work and at church, I grieved the loss of my son even more. During the past seven years, my goal was to get my

PhD. Now that I had it, it was a big letdown. I somehow felt that achieving my goal and finding my son would be simultaneous events; when I had achieved my goal I would also find my son.

I began to realize that I might never see him again. In the twelve years Buz and Philip had been missing, there had been absolutely no indication that either of them was still alive. There had been no word about them since that April day in 1970. Perhaps they drowned while sailing somewhere or died in some kind of accident.

The dean of the School of Nursing at USM, Dr. Jerri Laube, was a former departmental chairperson from Indiana University. She was a very capable person and easy to work with. She coached me in my new position as Director of Nursing Research and encouraged me to learn about funding opportunities for research. It was for this purpose that I attended a conference of the Gerontological Society of America in Boston. It was Thanksgiving break and I had the extra time to visit my sister Micki in Connecticut. While staying with her, I drove up to see Buz's brother, Joe, who lived about sixty miles from them. Joe and his wife, Alice, were happy to see me. As I entered their home, they took my coat and then looked at each other. Alice started out, "We have news for you. Mom has heard from Buz!"

Joe continued, "A couple weeks ago he called her and told her he was in Colorado and had a gift shop. She said she could hear a canary in the background. Philip was with him and he was fine, although she didn't speak with him. I think Buz called again after that. I'm not sure."

This is the first time anyone had heard from Buz in almost thirteen years. He was alive! And so was Philip!

Buz's entire family grieved over what he had done. They, too, had heard nothing and it had been very hard on Joe. Through the years, Alice and their three children sent me handmade gifts every Christmas —a gesture I appreciated more than they ever knew at the time.

It was difficult driving home that night, tears streaming down my face as wet snowflakes hit my windshield. A thousand thoughts swirled through my mind. They were alive! Alive and well! I now had to accept the fact that I had been deliberately deceived. I knew it, of course, but now it was staring me in the face. And I still didn't know if I would ever see my son again. And if I did, would he even know who I was?

I somehow managed to arrive safely at my sister's home. I shared the news with Micki and her husband, Dick. My youngest sister, Micki, helped and encouraged my search. She never gave up hope. I asked her about it, and she explained, "As a physical therapist, I work with people who are facing severe physical challenges. Motivation is critical and I'm good at motivating. I am used to working with problems that have no easy solutions. I'm not easily discouraged. I hate to give up. That is one reason, but mainly it is because I'm a mother and you are my sister. When Dori was born five months after Buz took Phil, I understood more of what you must be going through. Steven was born three years later after a difficult pregnancy. I had nightmares about children being abducted. Viv, I don't know how you survived, I'm not sure I could have."

Their neighbor, Ralph, joined us as we sat at the kitchen table strategizing what to do next. They suggested I call Child Find, an organization with a mission of locating lost children. I had recently heard of them, but had never contacted them. Micki found the number and helped me to place the call. I previously had not called because my anxiety level had been too high to tell the story again and to locate the supporting documents. With my sister's help, it was easy.

The lady on the other end of the telephone call gave me some practical advice. "You might consider hiring a private investigator. We have a list of those who specialize in this type of case. Call us back tomorrow if you would like this information."

Micki, Dick, Ralph, and I discussed it. Ralph was willing to lend me the money I needed. Ralph, a retired widower, was my sister's landlord as well as the neighbor downstairs. Through the years he had become a close friend of the family. I contacted a detective on the list they gave me and arranged to meet him the next day at a restaurant off the interstate somewhere between Connecticut and New York City.

I drove by myself. It was a ninety-minute drive from Hamden to the restaurant near the New York state border. When I met the detective, he looked like I pictured a private eye. A little rough on the edges, yet a smooth talker. We had lunch together and talked for over an hour. He asked a lot of questions about Buz, his personality, his work skills, jobs held, hobbies, and how he spent his leisure time. I told him about the times, when we were married, that I didn't know where he was or what he was doing. He asked me if I thought Buz was gay. I replied that I didn't know, but several people who knew him had asked me that same question.

Based on the information I gave him he conjectured that Buz would have returned to California by now and would probably be in Los Angeles—the place he had lived before and after we were married. He might be in the Hollywood area where he had once worked—perhaps as part of a gay community. I should consider that possibility.

"And, based on my past experience, once you are reunited with your son, there will be difficult times ahead of you. I will find him for you and tell you where he is. The rest is up to you. Remember, he is now fifteen years old."

He was ready to begin work. The fee was $2000, payable in advance. If I was interested, I could give him a check tomorrow. By now I was feeling quite uneasy with him and was glad when we got up to leave. He had invited me to lunch and now wanted $2000 as soon as possible. I thanked him and said I would think about it and get back with him by phone. He offered to pay for the meal and I let him.

Arriving back at my sister's home, I discussed it with Micki, Dick, and Ralph. The fee was way too much and I didn't like his demand to have it immediately. I called him the next day and told him I was no longer interested in hiring him.

I called Child Find again. They were not pleased to hear that the detective had asked for that much money in advance. They advised me not to hire him and gave me another telephone number. The new number was for an investigative agency based in Florida. Their fee was $400. As they were willing to take the information by phone, I went with them.

Barbara, my sister in Illinois, was interested in following up on the gift shop connection. A close friend of hers who owned a gift shop offered to look for him at trade shows. Another friend in Colorado was going to check out all of the gift shops in her area. My seventeen-year-old nephew, Craig, surprised and pleased that he had a cousin he didn't know existed (or didn't remember him), offered to personally search for Philip. Barbara also had a friend with political connections who she thought might be of some help.

Returning to Mississippi, I told some of my coworkers what had transpired. Very few people knew that I had a son. Now that I had specific information, I felt I wanted to let people know. A florist delivered a bouquet of flowers to my office from two graduate students with a card telling me they understood and were with me.

Someone suggested I make an appointment to visit the local FBI agent in Laurel, a logging town near Hattiesburg. It was well known that federal agents were present in the area to track drug smugglers coming from Mexico and the Caribbean. Suspicious activity was frequently reported in the area when small aircraft landed on open fields in secluded wooded areas.

The agent's office was located in a warehouse-type building in an unmarked room with no windows. I rang a bell in the hallway. A man let me in, escorted me to his desk, and listened to me, taking notes but not promising anything. I was surprised that the agent was even willing to talk with me. What I did not know at the time is that the Federal Missing Children's Act of 1982 had been passed, allowing the Federal Bureau of Investigation to become involved in such cases. It was now January 1983. Nothing had changed for me. Philip was still missing. Yet everything had changed!

# 14
# The Flood

Philip would soon be sixteen years old and learning to drive. In a few months I would be able check to see if a driver's license had been issued to him. Now that I knew they were alive and in the United States, I had hope.

I decided to try placing a missing person ad in a magazine—a publication read by school teachers. Philip would be in school somewhere.

I placed an ad in *Instructor* magazine with a picture of Philip at age three and another of Buz and me holding Philip as a baby. It read:

> *MISSING 16-YEAR-OLD SON*
>
> *Philip Hayes, Born 1967*
>
> *Blonde hair, blue eyes, abducted by father in 1970*
>
> *Possibly in Europe 1970-73, then in U.S. under new name*
>
> *Anyone having information*
>
> *Call Toll Free Child Find, Inc.*
>
> *800- ________*
>
> *Case No. 2227*

I was hoping someone might recognize Buz. Ralph loaned me $1087 for the ad.

April 2 marked the thirteenth anniversary of the abduction. Easter was coming soon, and I made arrangements to see my mother and oldest sister, Adeline, who were vacationing in Florida. Ralph was there also. It was a short two days, but a nice break and an opportunity to talk with them about all that had transpired the past few months.

There was more drama to come.

A few days later, back at the university, a staff member came into my office, advising me, "You better leave! It's raining hard. In an hour or so you won't be able to get home. Everyone is leaving."

I was working on a project and stayed at my desk a little longer to finish what I was writing. I was among the last to leave the building.

I soon realized I had waited too long. I could hardly see through the downpour to locate my car. Fortunately, by the time I was nearing home the rain stopped. As I turned off the highway, I could see the road ahead of me was flooded. But further on it was not. Thinking I could make it, I turned off the road and drove forward trying to reach the high, dry ground. That was a mistake! Water began to seep through the floor from below. I quickly grabbed the important papers on the seat next to me, and holding them over my head, got out and began walking toward the side of the road.

I heard someone shouting, "Don't move! Stay where you are! Don't move! I will come and get you!"

I froze where I was standing, and two men, one driving a large truck, rescued me and drove me home. The apartment complex where I lived was next to a creek. My door was open and my neighbor and several other men were moving furniture around to minimize water damage as the water was coming in. In about an hour the water receded and we all went to our apartments.

About one a.m., I awakened to pounding on the door. "Get out! We're being evacuated!"

I got out and joined my neighbors who were gathered on the lawn in a high area. We were told the dam above the creek had broken and was about to flood the entire area. We waited a couple of hours until we were told everything was under control. I slept the rest of the night in my upstairs bedroom.

The sun came out the next day and the floodwaters receded. I walked down the road about a half mile to pick up my car. I was shocked to see a steep drop-off and a fast-flowing creek next to the car. If I had continued walking yesterday, I would have walked right into the creek. I had heard on the news that a man had drowned in the same creek yesterday as he was washed away by the floodwaters. I knew it easily could have been me. God was with me.

One morning, about a week later, I was sitting in my office chatting with Mary, a colleague who had come to say hello. Our conversation was interrupted by a phone call. "Hello, is this Vivian Hayes?"

"Yes, it is."

"This is Dr. Larry Barr calling from California. I have your son Philip here. Would you like to speak with him?"

"Yes! I have been searching for him for years."

# 15
# Hollywood

I think I was in a state of shock. I motioned to Mary that it was a very important call I had to take. She left the office immediately and I sat down to continue the call.

I heard a deep voice, "Hello."

"Philip, I love you. I've been searching for you for years."

"My Dad didn't mean to hurt you."

I don't recall what else we said. It was a short conversation and Philip turned the phone over to Dr. Barr. Dr. Barr told me that Philip's father had told Philip of my whereabouts yesterday and gave him my parents' address and phone number in Illinois. Prior to that, all he had been told was, "Your mother died."

Dr. Barr had called my mother to get my current number. I told him I would be in California as soon as possible. My colleague Mary and Bill, the admissions counselor in the office next door, were excited about the good news and helped me process the information.

"You must leave today," they advised. "Take the next flight out."

I called my mother and told her the good news. She had just received the phone call from Dr. Barr asking for my phone number, so she was not surprised. She would meet me in Los Angeles as soon as we could both get there.

Less than ten hours later, I was at LAX getting off the plane. Philip was to meet me at the gate and would recognize me as the woman in the blue dress. There were several women on that flight wearing blue dresses, but he quickly recognized me.

He said, "Are you Vivian?"

I looked at him and assured him that I was; then we embraced.

Philip looked much the same as he did when he was three. The big blue eyes and the sweet expression on his face were unmistakably his. His hair was still curly, but now light brown. He was somewhat in a daze as he looked at me carefully. I was in a daze myself.

I had always thought I would be the one to find him. But he found me. It was better this way.

For a moment, I thought. "How do I know this is my son?" Then I saw him walk. As a child he had a distinctive walk and had worn corrective shoes. His feet still toed inward as did mine. I had no doubt that this was my son.

I sat down and got acquainted with Dr. Larry Barr, a school psychologist at Happy Valley School in Ojai where Philip had been a boarding student. When Philip dropped out of school, Larry continued to counsel him and provide tutoring. They became good friends and Philip was often a guest at the home of Larry and his wife Diane. When Buz told our son the truth about me, his mother, Philip immediately rode his bicycle to Larry's home and told him what had happened. Our son was shocked to learn that his name was Hayes, not Hansen and that his mother was alive. I would learn more about this later.

Philip had with him a picture of me that his father had given him. He stared at it, then looked at me, and back at the picture again. I stared at him. He was a beautiful young man with a sweet, innocent look on his face. Larry did most of the talking, filling me in on details. My mother soon arrived on another flight. Then my dear friends, Mary Keene and her husband arrived. Mary had worked with me at Kaiser and had shared my burden through the years. I had called her and other friends earlier in the day to tell them the good news. After talking with Philip and Larry a little longer, we all left. My Mom and I went to a local hotel and Philip, now called Phil, went home with Larry.

My whole world was shaken, and so was Phil's. Buz had long ago changed his own name to Otto Hansen and was now working as a gardener in Beverly Hills. That made sense to me as he had majored in botany and chemistry and always loved plants.

My mother and I met Larry and Phil the next day for dinner. Larry then dropped the three of us off at a hotel in Hollywood where we spent the night. It was arranged for Buz to meet us there the next morning and take me out to breakfast. Larry would come at the same time to take Phil home with him.

Larry was there at 8:30 a.m. and all of us waited downstairs for Buz. I was not sure how my mother would greet him, because she was clearly very angry with him. Her assessment of his personality years ago was, "He is selfish!"

Buz drove up in an old station wagon with a lawn mower and garden tools in the back. He seemed quite thin, had white hair, and was wearing old jeans and a T-shirt. Not the handsome, well-dressed man I once knew, but still charming when he smiled and called out, "Hi, I haven't seen you in a long time! Hop in!"

I smiled, greeted him, and went to the other side and jumped in—just as I had done years ago when we were dating. He didn't miss a beat.

My mother greeted Buz pleasantly, saying something like, "It's nice to see you again."

Phil talked with his dad for a minute or two and off we went.

As he drove, we talked about his work as a gardener and how he specialized in cultivating roses. He was now living in North Hollywood. I told him what I was doing.

We talked about our common interest—our son. Phil had been in a private boarding school in Ojai, California, but was now living with him. After Buz broke up with his partner, Samuel, who was paying the fees, he could no longer afford to send him there. I remembered Samuel from years ago. He had visited us in our home in San Diego when Phil was only two. He arrived in a Rolls Royce and I was told he was a very important person at a major Hollywood studio. After Philip left the boarding school, Larry Barr hired someone to tutor him and he was able to pass the California Proficiency Certificate exam. Phil was now a high school graduate at sixteen. They had moved around a lot, but Phil was very bright and, overall, did well in school.

This was all so strange. It was as if nothing had ever happened between us.

We chatted while we had breakfast. The conversation eventually became more serious. I told Buz I forgave him.

He retorted back, "I forgive you, too," as if he had done nothing wrong and didn't need forgiveness—it was *I* who needed it. We both saw that we were getting angry and changed the tone of the conversation quickly.

He told me of some of his problems of the last six months. He had been admitted to a critical care unit for chest pain in December. The good news is that it was not a heart attack.

He told me he was gay. I said I knew it. I had suspected it for a long time, but did not know for sure until Larry told me two days ago. Now I could tell by looking at him. His mannerisms, way of dressing, and speech patterns had changed. The difference, to me, was remarkable and not at all attractive.

He told me that his partner and soul mate, Samuel, a successful Hollywood writer, had recently committed suicide, and it was hard on him. Added to that, Phil wanted to be more independent and was sometimes critical of his father. We both smiled at that. I listened and did not ask any questions.

Buz did not like Larry Barr, but nevertheless acknowledged that our son did. So he allowed Phil to spend considerable time with Larry and his wife.

I told him that Phil's first words to me were, "My father didn't mean to hurt you." Buz cried, and I accepted that as an apology. He said he wanted to give himself up many times, but did not know how to do it without ending up in jail. He was scared and kept on moving.

Then the story came out.

When he left Los Angeles in 1970, he flew to Amsterdam where he stayed for a while. After a short time he ran out of money and returned to a US territory, the Virgin Islands. There he was able to secure the social security number of a deceased man by the name of Otto Hansen.

"It was easy to do. It was the time of the Vietnam War and draft dodgers were taking on new identities and moving to Canada."

He gave his passport and other papers to a friend for safekeeping and never saw the friend or the papers again. He wasn't at all happy with that. There were some photos of Phil he did keep and eventually wanted to give to me.

After working in the Virgin Islands for a while, he moved to Florida. There he got a good job in a lab—until he saw someone he had worked with in California. He quit that job immediately. It was hard keeping a job, he said, because as soon as he saw someone he knew, he had to quit and move on.

At one point he designed and built sets for the TV program *Day of Discovery*, a religious program produced by members of the Reformed Church in America. He laughed at that because we had originally met at Hope College––a college of that denomination. At some point he left Florida and moved from place to place until he returned to California.

He did most of the talking. I was to get more details later, but this was enough for now. He dropped me off at the hotel and drove away. I joined Mom at the hotel.

Mom was glad to be leaving *that hotel.* "Did you know there were prostitutes coming and going last night? When I checked in for us last night, the clerk thought I was a *Madam*. Let's get out of here!"

Mom, Phil, and I left the hotel and went to the McCauleys. They had invited their daughter Norma and her family for dinner. Norma baked a cake that said, "*Happiness is Philip*."

While we were there, Phil called a friend, Esther Moore, in Columbia, Mississippi, to tell her he had found his mother. She had been like a grandmother to him when he had lived with her for a short time. Columbia was only thirty-two miles from where I lived in Hattiesburg. What a coincidence!

The next morning, Mom left for the airport and Phil and I went to church at Trinity. Phil's comment as we drove into the parking lot in San Pedro was, "You mean this is the church I would have attended, if I had lived with you?"

A few people at church knew I had found Philip, but most had not yet heard. Rex Varvais was the first to greet us in the narthex. He was delighted to see me again, and his jaw dropped when I introduced my son to him. What a surprise! Rex had known little Philip well. He owned a gas station and auto repair shop and had kept my blue Plymouth running all those years.

Pastor Paul Anderson and Greg Goble led the church service. I had known Greg as a quiet teenager. He was now a tall, self-assured, handsome young man with a beautiful voice. Today he sang and led worship. Greg greeted us publicly, but could tell that Phil was not ready for a big welcome and said no more. It was a quiet time of rejoicing for all. I knew it was not easy for Phil, so we left quickly after the service was over.

1983. Phil and Vivian shortly after their reunion.
(Photo by Norma McCauley.)

## 16
## The Strife Is O'er

The next day I was on a flight back to Mississippi. I was exhausted and tears of joy welled up in my eyes as I walked down the long flight of stairs to my connecting flight. I began singing a hymn to myself.

> The strife is o'er, the battle done;
> Now is the Victor's triumph won!
> Now be the song of praise begun.
> Al-le-lu-ia![10]

The spiritual battle that had been going on for more than a decade was over. Light had entered the darkness as the truth gradually came out. During the past several days I had learned some of what transpired during those missing years. Some of my worst fears had, in fact, come to pass. It was hard hearing all the details over such a short period of time, and it was difficult to see Buz the way he was. He was thin and living a gay lifestyle, barely making enough money to pay bills—so unnecessary and such a waste. I was angry with him, but I also pitied him and had compassion on him. He was a broken man. Phil had survived. Larry explained to me that, because Phil is very bright, he was able to figure things out and take care of himself. Another psychologist friend described Phil as being resilient and resourceful. He was all of these and, yes, he had his special angels watching over him—the angels that always behold the face of God.

One of the first things I did on returning to Mississippi was to contact Esther Moore in Columbia. One day after work I went to see her. It was just a forty-five-minute drive from campus, mostly through picturesque wooded areas. She had talked with Phil a couple times on the phone so was up-to-date on what had happened. Prior to that, she had not been in contact with him for years and often thought of him. Her husband had died a few years ago, and she was living alone.

Phil's bicycle was still on the front porch of the old frame house where they lived. His bedroom still had the ceramic plaque on the door that said "Phil's Room." She went into a cupboard, took out a ceramic figurine he had made, and gave it to me.

"Just when he was beginning to make friends in the neighborhood, Buz came and took him away," she said. "We wanted him to stay with us, but Buz would not allow it. I had previously met Buz and did not believe that his son's mother was dead. I told Phil to keep asking about his mother—ask where she is buried. All Phil was ever told is that his mother died in a 'terrible accident'—never any details."

Esther and her husband clearly loved the ten-year-old child they had with them for almost a year, and I was grateful to her for that. She told me the story of how Phil came to them.

"One day I received a phone call from my son, George, in Florida. 'I have a ten-year-old boy here with me, the son of my roommate. It's too dangerous for him to be here. Can you take him for a while? I'm going to put him on the next flight to New Orleans.'We went to the airport in New Orleans that evening," she continued. "When Phil got off the plane, he looked like a little lost boy. All he had with him was a small gym bag with a pair of swim trunks. That was all. We took him home with us."

"The first thing we did was to go out and buy him some clothes. We had not gone to church in years, but for Phil we started going to the Methodist church again. We bought him a nice suit to wear on special occasions and the pastor even let him light the candles in church. We enrolled him in school."

"He spent a lot of time with my husband, whom he called Grandpa. Grandpa taught him how to enjoy the outdoors and shoot a BB gun. We both missed Phil very much when he left. Now I'm glad he's found you."

"My son George wants to talk with you," continued Esther. "He lives in a house we built on some farmland just out of town."

I told her to have George call me.

On my way home all I could think of was, "Truth is stranger than fiction." The information I was getting day by day was overwhelming.

I met with George the following week at a restaurant in Hattiesburg. He brought with him an envelope with photos of Phil when he was about eight or ten years old and living with them in Florida. George was Buz's partner at the time and helped care for Phil. Yes, he knew of the abduction and, at Buz's request, made a phone call to my sister in Connecticut, attempting to get information about my family.

Then I recalled my sister telling me about some strange phone calls she had received some years ago. It was probably George.

George told me that their relationship ended when Buz became interested in another man. It was rather sudden and he was deeply hurt by it. He warned me to be very careful with any future dealings I had with Buz.

It was surreal. Here we were, sitting in a restaurant talking about a man we had both loved, and he had jilted both of us. George continued the conversation, telling little stories of Phil's childhood, leaving the photos with me to keep. It was his way of saying, "I'm sorry." Afterward, all I could think of was, "Lord, do I have to forgive *him*, too? It's enough that I have to forgive my ex-husband. But do I have to forgive all of his crazy friends—those who knew what he was doing, and could have blown his cover at any time?"

But I was grateful for what George had done for Phil. He loved him and gave him some stability. Without his intervention my son would not have had a year with George's parents—a good year. And who knows what might have happened in Florida.

On returning to the campus of the University of Southern Mississippi, I was asked if I would be willing to meet with a university staff reporter, Roger Brinegar, for a possible story about my finding my son.

Roger and I sat in my office in the nursing building and talked for a couple hours. He was empathetic, and I felt he would get the story straight. He agreed to use little information about Buz or Phil, as that was still a sensitive area. It would be mostly about me, my search for my son, and how I was able to cope with the uncertainty. He promised to let me read it before it was published. He did that, and I made no changes. It was an accurate account of what I had told him.

The story was to appear on the front page of the *Hattiesburg American* that Sunday: "Mom Discovers Son After 13 Years."[11] That morning I asked the pastor of the Presbyterian Church I attended if I could briefly tell my story from the pulpit, as people would soon see it in the paper. I spoke for a minute or two about my son who had been lost and now found. This was a modern version of the story of the Prodigal Son.[12] I invited them to rejoice with me.

Different versions of the article appeared in several newspapers in the state. I received a call from a writer in Jackson interested in doing a movie version of the story. I was not ready for that and did not follow up on it. Two other writers inquired, but it did not seem wise to allow them to do a story. A couple of women called asking for assistance in helping to find their missing children. I didn't know how to help them except to tell them what I had done. One of the women came to see me in my office and I listened to her story. I wished there was more I could have done.

I sent copies of the article to friends who had been praying for us through the years and heard from many of them. I sent the article to Child Find Inc., the US Passport office, and several other people and organizations who had helped me through the years. I heard from all of them thanking me for the story. They remarked that it is not often a missing child story has a happy ending.

I received a personal response from Senator Bayh. It concluded with, "My hope for you and your son is to regain those lost years and grow with each other into the mother/son relationship our Lord meant you to have."[13]

Developing a relationship with my son was not easy for either of us after so many years had elapsed. There was an immediate bonding, but a rocky road for both of us. This was an uncharted course.

As soon as the academic year came to a close, I returned to California for a week.

I stayed with the McCauleys again. Phil was living with his father and had a job at a little coffee shop/cafe in a mall. I visited him briefly at work. The next day he took me to Universal Studios amusement park; it was a fun day for both of us. He was such a sweet, gentle person. All I could think of was the verse of scripture, "You are My beloved Son, in You I am well-pleased."[14]

Buz had done many things right in raising him. Many people had, in fact, raised him, but Buz had been careful to leave him with good people—with George and George's parents, faculty and staff at Happy Valley School, with parents of his classmates and with Larry Barr. It could have been worse. Much worse.

The next day, Phil and I, along with Bob, a classmate of his, went to the Galleria Mall in Sherman Oaks—the home of the Valley girls. Yes, the girls really do talk like that. We walked around, took pictures, and had something to eat—just hanging out.

Phil wanted me to see his room and spend the night at their apartment. I accepted the invitation, and the plan was for Buz to spend the night elsewhere.

He was proud to show me his room —a typical teenager's room with posters on the wall and a guitar propped up next to his bed, a mattress on the floor. It was a cozy room, a partitioned portion of a larger bedroom. Buz called me into the kitchen and told me he was now in therapy and had changed his name back to Hayes. He took out a shoebox filled with photos and memorabilia from Phil's childhood: a Boy Scout scarf, letters from Phil while he was at camp, a newspaper clipping of Phil's Florida kindergarten class, and photos of him at different ages. He told me stories about his childhood, and then gave the box to me.

I thought, "Is that it? I have a box of pictures. Is that all I have of thirteen years? A small box? I missed all of those years with my son and all I have is a box!"

Both of us were beginning to experience a mixture of anger and sadness, and we knew it. Buz left quickly and said he would not be back until tomorrow noon.

Early the next morning I left to have breakfast and drove to Ojai. Phil was to have breakfast with Larry and meet me in Ojai. From there we went to Happy Valley School, where Phil had been a student and Larry was on the counseling staff. Phil had already told his friends he had found his mother. Now he wanted to introduce me. I met them and some of the staff. Before I left I spent some time with the principal and had my first and only parent-teacher conference.

God is good. Little by little, those lost years were being restored.

We drove to Malibu to meet his friend, Jamie, and his mother and stepfather. Both were successful writers in the movie and TV industry. His stepfather also owned a gift shop and had sold ceramic items handcrafted by Buz.

I realized that's where the scenario of owning a gift shop came from!

He told Phil to make an audio recording of his thoughts and keep it for a book he might eventually want to write. "Your thoughts and feelings now will not be the same later on, so record them now. This is a love story. Both your father and mother love you."

Plans were made for the summer. Larry, acting on my behalf, had already helped Phil change his name to Hayes on his certificates and school records. He was now helping him get his driver's license and buy a car.

The plan was for Phil to come to live with me in Hattiesburg and attend USM. We would pack up his car and drive to Hattiesburg together. After he was settled there, he would fly alone to Connecticut and Chicago to meet relatives he didn't know existed three months ago.

Before I left California I visited Trinity again. I was happy to see Dave Churness, someone I had not seen since I left California nine years earlier. His wife Barbara had died four years ago of breast cancer. The last time I saw Barbara and Dave was in the Trinity bookstore, where they had both volunteered. I remember their two children, Sarah, age four, and Peter, age six, playing in a corner under their mother's watchful eyes. Now she was gone. My heart went out to all of them.

# 17
# Change

Phil and I drove from California to Mississippi, carrying all of his belongings in a small trunk tied to the top of his little Datsun 1200. We made a stop in Phoenix to stay with friends while an overheating radiator was repaired. Then we were on our way, listening to Phil's favorite rock music on tapes as we drove. One of my favorite new songs was David Bowie's *Changes*.[15] I could identify with those words.

When we were somewhere in the middle of Texas, I decided I wanted to lie down and stretch out on the back seat of the car. Because the speakers in the back were blaring in my ears, I asked Phil to please turn down the volume. I didn't realize the control for the speakers was next to me in the backseat. As he turned around to comply with my request, he lost control of the car. The car swerved back and forth as Phil tried to gain control of it again. He was almost successful, but the weight of the trunk strapped to the roof was too much for the small car. We gradually went off the pavement and onto the dirt shoulder. I thought, "Come on, Phil, we'll make it!" But we rocked back and forth in the soft, almost sandy, dirt, slowly turning over.

All I could think of as we were turning upside down was, "Oh, no, Lord! Not something else!" I was not afraid, because I didn't think either of us would be injured. I just looked at it as a huge inconvenience—one we surely didn't need at this time.

Neither of us was injured. The car was turned upsidedown like a turtle with its legs in the air. Since neither of us was wearing seat belts we found ourselves sitting on what was once the ceiling. With the engine no longer running, the stereo was now blaring out louder than ever with David Bowie singing, "Ch-Ch-Change!" More change than I could handle right now.

People witnessing it immediately came to our rescue and turned off the stereo. Here we were—in the middle of a desert. We had not seen any other car for miles, yet as soon as we turned over, a group of people were there to help us. Some Good Samaritans took us to a motel in the next town and had our car towed to a nearby garage. It wasn't until after it was over that I realized we could have been seriously injured or killed had we been going faster or been in heavy traffic.

It was Phil's first car and it was wrecked! The car, the trunk, and its contents were all that he owned. He really, *really*, wanted to keep the car. The garage mechanic understood and said he would try to repair it so it was drivable.

In the meantime, all we could do was lie around in our motel room and watch TV. We both ached all over, so it was a good thing.

It also gave us time to get reacquainted. Phil told me about another accident he had been in a few months before we were reunited. He was riding his Vespa motor scooter when a car made a left-hand turn in front of him.

"I hit the car head on and flew thirty-five feet into the air. I totally cleared the car, went all the way above the car, and landed on the ground and rolled. I was not injured except for a quarter-inch cut on my knee. I didn't even need any stitches."

God had miraculously preserved him. It reminded me of the recent close call I had in the flood. Had I taken a few more steps in the direction I was headed I could have drowned in the swift current of the creek. But that did not happen. The Lord was watching over both of us.

After two days of rest, the repairman came to the motel to tell us our car was ready. No windshield of the proper size was available to replace the shattered one, so he wired a larger one in place and secured it with duct tape. He charged very little for the repairs and off we went.

Now it looked like the car had wings. The side windows were also broken in the crash, so the car had no windows, allowing the wind to whip through the car as we drove away. When we stopped at a gas station, the attendants saw us and laughed. "It looks like "Chitty Chitty Bang Bang!"

We continued on through Texas, stopped overnight at a family-owned motel somewhere in Louisiana, and finally on to Mississippi.

A week after our arrival in Mississippi, Phil took his ACT exam and was admitted as a freshman at the university where I worked. He went on to spend the rest of the summer with relatives on the East Coast and the Midwest, then back again to Mississippi. It was a time of adjustment for both of us. I was not used to having a sixteen-year-old son, and he was not used to having a mother, but we somehow managed. Phil was able to visit with Grandma Moore and George in Columbia whenever he wanted to. We seemed to be in the right place at that time.

At the end of the semester in December, he returned to California, where he felt more comfortable. I spent Christmas in California and made plans to move there in February. After only two years at USM, and sooner than I had expected, I left my faculty position. God had been good to me by putting me in such a supportive environment at that time. I will never forget the kindness of so many people.

I moved back to San Pedro where I could again be part of the Trinity Lutheran Church family. Phil moved in with his dad for a short time, and then various places, until we helped him find housing in Santa Barbara, where he enrolled in a community college. I found temporary work with Kaiser, my former employer, until I could find a more permanent position. I was soon offered a faculty position at the University of Southern California in the newly formed Department of Nursing.

In church I became reacquainted with Dave Churness, and it wasn't long before we were engaged. I had known Barbara, his wife, and had once thought, "Someday, I'd like to marry someone like him." Dave had been widowed for five years now, and with the help of two grandmothers and people from church, he and his children had managed to survive. Sarah and Peter were delighted about the upcoming marriage, as were our friends. Dave and I joked that the church people were happy because two problems (Dave and Vivian) were solved at one time.

Dave had another son, Emory, who was twenty-two years old, living in Wisconsin. Dave's three children plus my son meant we were an instant family of six. A huge change for me, but one I had longed for.

It was a good match. Dave was a pharmacist so we had our medical backgrounds in common. Dave was interested in missions and had at one time considered being a missionary doctor. We shared a common faith and had many friends in common. We could sit for hours and talk.

My son, Phil, and Dave's son, Peter, later moved near the University of Southern California where they were enrolled as students; and Sarah went to college in Valparaiso, Indiana. From time to time, Emory visited, or we visited him. All of our children have done well in life. What pleases us most is that they get along well with each other and enjoy the times they are together.

Buz was diagnosed with AIDS and died in 1992. I had long suspected he was HIV positive. That was just a guess, as I had never asked. I also never asked him what prompted him to tell Phil the truth about me. My hunch is that there were many factors, but underlying them all was the fact that he knew he was HIV positive and might not live for long. I will never know.

One day, five years after Dave and I were married, I received a phone call from Christine Anker, a friend who had known Buz. She was excited and went on, "I just saw an article written by Buz in a magazine called *Health World.*[16] He wrote about an algae food supplement he was taking for AIDS. In the article he gives a sort of public confession about how he took his son. The title of the article is 'The Users Testimonials: Victory over AIDS'."

Then she read it to me over the phone:

> *Born and raised in New England, I started college on the east coast . . . and spent 7 years in 5 or 6 schools to graduate with a degree in botany. I worked at . . . and got married and had a son.*
>
> *When my son was 3, I took a thirteen- year vacation with him, leaving behind a note saying, 'Gone to the zoo.' We had a great time with two birds and a faithful schnauzer, Schultz. When my son was 16, and shortly after the suicide of my Emmy-award–winning soul-mate, I returned my son to his mother, and spent some time with my mother.*

*Well, I've taken . . . read, meditated, detoxified and did everything that appealed to me; then I was diagnosed with ARC (AIDS-Related Complex) in December 1985 by Dr. . . . with T4s at 193, swollen lymph glands . . .*

Then he went on to say how taking the food supplement for a year brought his T4 count up with no major health problems since then.

Have I forgiven him? Yes, long ago, for four reasons. First, I do it for my own sake. If I did not forgive, I would be carrying around a big weight and would not be free to live life to the fullest.

Second, I do it for my son's sake. His life has been difficult enough without my harboring continued resentment against his father.

Third, I do it because God commanded us to forgive others as we ourselves have been forgiven. We pray, "Forgive us our sins, as we forgive those who sin against us."[17]

Fourth, it is part of living in grace and something I *want* to do, because I myself have been forgiven.

We saw Buz from time to time and Dave was very kind to him. At times, when I was upset with him about something, Dave would remind me, "Be nice!"

Before he died, Buz thanked Dave for all he had done for his son, taking care of him and helping to educate him.

# Epilogue

It is now 2013. Phil is an artist and a successful animator for a TV show. He has a beautiful wife and two daughters, ages eight and ten. They are good parents. We see them often, as they live nearby. Peter, Sarah, and Emory live farther away in other states, but we keep in close touch with each other. We have a total of seven grandchildren.

After retiring from USC, I reconnected with friends in India and the mission hospital where I once served as a missionary. Since 2007 I have taken nine trips to India serving as a Consultant in Nursing Education to the Church of South India. I have mostly been revising or writing nursing textbooks for nurses in India. While there, I enjoy visiting with old and new friends, encouraging them in their Christian faith and in their work. I love the country of India and feel blessed to be able to continue my relationship with the people there. My husband, Dave, who doesn't travel to India with me, prays for me and encourages me while I travel and while I am at home writing. I have also been able to pursue a lifelong hobby of mine—music. I continue to take clarinet lessons and also teach a number of young students.

I can honestly say that these are now the best years of my life. The Lord has been with me as He promised and has restored the lost years a thousand fold. I often think of the verse of scripture someone gave me to read years ago.

And I will restore to you the years that the locust hath eaten.[18]

He has done that.

## Notes

[1] Paul Simon, "Bridge over Troubled Water," Performed by Paul Simon and Art Garfunkel (Columbia Records, 1970).

[2] Hebrews 13:5 (ESV).

[3] Matthew 18:5,10 (NIV).

[4] Romans 8:38-39 (NIV).

[5] Bob Hilliard (lyrics) and Sammy Fain (music), "Dear Hearts and Gentle People" (1949, Recorded by various artists).

[6] Paul Tournier, *Escape from Loneliness,* translated by Paul Gilmour. (Philadelphia: Westminster Press, 1962), 1.

[7] John F. Shea (lyrics), Rev. Michael J. Shea (music), "Notre Dame Victory March" (University of Notre Dame, 1928, 1956: MPL Communications, Distributed by Hal Leonard Corp.).

[8] John 10:4-5 (NIV).

[9] *Instructor*, Vol. XCII, No. 9, May 1983, 12.

[10] "The Strife Is O'er, the Battle Done," author unknown, 1695, tr. Francis Pott, 1832–1909.

[11] Roger Brinegar, "Mom Discovers Son After 13 Years," *Hattiesburg American,* May 8, 1983.

[12] Luke 15:11-31.

[13] Birch Bayh, personal correspondence to Vivian Hayes, (Washington DC, October 21, 1983).

14 Mark 1:11 (NASB).

15 David Bowie, "Changes" (1971, album *Hunky Dory*).

16 Robert Hayes, "The Users Testimonials; Victory Over AIDS," *Health World, Special Edition, Chorella* (Burlingame, CA: Health World, Inc., 1989), 66–67.

17 Luke 11:4 (nlt).

18 Joel 2:25 (KJV).